"In *Truth We Can Touch*, Tim Chester makes a [...] cals to recover an understanding of baptism an[...] promise that comes to us in physical form. Deeply biblical and yet eminently practical, this book provides an alternative to a theology of the word limited to our heads. God's word in Christ comes to us not only in preaching but also in baptism and at the table. As embodied creatures, we embrace God's promises in touch and taste, with delight and praise. This accessible and winsome book is a joy!"

J. Todd Billings, Gordon H. Girod Research Professor of Reformed Theology, Western Theological Seminary; author, *Remembrance, Communion, and Hope*

"This is hands down the best book on the sacraments I've read—warm, compelling, eye-opening, and saturated in gospel encouragement. I hadn't realized how much I needed it."

Sam Allberry, Ravi Zacharias International Ministries; author, *Why Bother with Church?*

"In this delightful book, Chester reminds us that baptism and Communion are God's gifts to us that convey the gospel and grace in powerful ways. As a Baptist I would put some things differently, but I celebrate and rejoice in the main thesis set forth by Chester. Baptism and Communion are central in the New Testament, and something is wrong if they are neglected or ignored by us. Take up and read and be instructed, challenged, and—most of all—encouraged by the gospel, which is displayed so beautifully in baptism and the Eucharist."

Thomas R. Schreiner, James Buchanan Harrison Professor of New Testament Interpretation and Professor of Biblical Theology, The Southern Baptist Theological Seminary

"After reading Tim Chester's *Truth We Can Touch*, I sent our pastoral staff a message: 'Add this book to our reading list for our interns, and add it to our book nook.' Chester is one of our favorite writers, and his books have blessed our local church. Once again, he combines theological clarity with gospel warmth, conveying the beauty of Christ to the reader. By reading this accessible book, you will value baptism and Communion more, and you will be moved to worship the Savior as you consider Chester's explanation of baptism as the embodiment of our union with Christ and the Lord's Supper as the embodiment of our communion with Christ."

Tony Merida, Pastor, Imago Dei Church, Raleigh, North Carolina

"At last, here is a great evangelical book on the sacraments. I have longed for such a book for years, one that is deep yet accessible, theologically robust and biblically grounded, and—perhaps most of all—one that touches the heart with wise pastoral application. This is a valuable resource for all ministers and a treasure for all God's people. I cannot commend it highly enough—a delight from beginning to end."

Melvin Tinker, Senior Minister, St John Newland, Hull, United Kingdom; author, *Language, Symbols, and Sacraments*

"The sacraments are integral to the history of redemption, yet the evangelical church has tragically neglected them as secondary and nonessential. Tim Chester sets baptism and the Lord's Supper vividly in their biblical and historical contexts. Superbly written, easily accessible to a wide readership, rooted in Scripture and the theology of the Reformation, this book can be a catalyst for widespread recovery of the supreme blessing God gives through his appointed signs."

Robert Letham, Professor of Systematic and Historical Theology, Union School of Theology

TRUTH
WE CAN TOUCH

Other Crossway Books by Tim Chester

Everyday Church: Gospel Communities on Mission, with Steve Timmis

Good News to the Poor: Social Involvement and the Gospel

A Meal with Jesus: Discovering Grace, Community, and Mission around the Table

Reforming Joy: A Conversation between Paul, the Reformers, and the Church Today

Total Church: A Radical Reshaping around Gospel and Community, with Steve Timmis

Why the Reformation Still Matters, with Michael Reeves

You Can Change: God's Transforming Power for Our Sinful Behavior and Negative Emotions

TRUTH
WE CAN TOUCH

*How Baptism and Communion
Shape Our Lives*

Tim Chester

Foreword by Sinclair B. Ferguson

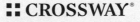

:: **CROSSWAY**®

WHEATON, ILLINOIS

Cover design: Jeff Miller, Faceout Studios

Cover image: Shutterstock

First printing 2020

Printed in the United States of America

Unless otherwise indicated, Scripture quotations are from the ESV® Bible (The Holy Bible, English Standard Version®), copyright © 2001 by Crossway, a publishing ministry of Good News Publishers. Used by permission. All rights reserved.

Scripture references marked NIV are taken from The Holy Bible, New International Version®, NIV®. Copyright © 1973, 1978, 1984, 2011 by Biblica, Inc.™ Used by permission. All rights reserved worldwide.

All emphases in Scripture quotations have been added by the author.

Trade paperback ISBN: 978-1-4335-6657-8
ePub ISBN: 978-1-4335-6660-8
PDF ISBN: 978-1-4335-6658-5
Mobipocket ISBN: 978-1-4335-6659-2

Library of Congress Cataloging-in-Publication Data

Names: Chester, Tim, author. | Ferguson, Sinclair B., writer of foreword.
Title: Truth we can touch: how baptism and communion shape our lives / Tim Chester; foreword by Sinclair Ferguson.
Description: Wheaton, Illinois: Crossway, [2020] | Includes bibliographical references and indexes.
Identifiers: LCCN 2019021332 (print) | LCCN 2019981581 (ebook) | ISBN 9781433566578 (trade paperback) | ISBN 9781433566592 (mobi) | ISBN 9781433566608 (epub) | ISBN 9781433566585 (pdf)
Subjects: LCSH: Sacraments. | Baptism. | Lord's Supper. | Christian life.
Classification: LCC BV800 .C523 2020 (print) | LCC BV800 (ebook) | DDC 264/.9—dc23
LC record available at https://lccn.loc.gov/2019021332
LC ebook record available at https://lccn.loc.gov/2019981581

Crossway is a publishing ministry of Good News Publishers.

VP		30	29	28	27	26	25	24	23	22	21	20
15	14	13	12	11	10	9	8	7	6	5	4	3	2	1

CONTENTS

FOREWORD

It is a privilege to introduce *Truth We Can Touch* and to commend it to you. This is a much more important book than its size might suggest, because it will help you to understand and enjoy two of Christ's special gifts to you—baptism and the Lord's Supper. Reading it reminded me of two incidents in my life.

The first was a conversation I had years ago with a doctoral student from the Far East. I knew him as "Timothy." But one day, when I felt I had come to know him well enough, I asked him, "Timothy, what's your *real* name?" He smiled and said, "Timothy." I smiled back, knowing he would see that I wasn't convinced this was the whole truth! "Come on, tell me, what is your real name?" Again, he replied, "Timothy." So, I tried a different maneuver. "What is the name your parents registered for you?" This time he responded with his native Asian name. Despite feeling we were in the endgame of a little chess match and that somehow he had a secret move up his sleeve, I said, "So *that's your real name!*" "No," he said—and then theologically checkmated me! "Timothy is my real name. *That's the name I was given when I was baptized.*"

Timothy taught me a great lesson that day. The name you were given at your baptism is even more important than the name by which your birth was registered. Timothy's baptismal name had not changed Timothy's heart any more than his ethnic name had. But since the day of his baptism, it had reminded him who he was as a Christian and had called him to live in the light of that.

The conversation left me wondering if Timothy was in the minority of Christians—someone who understood his baptism well enough for it to have an ongoing significance for him every day of his life.

You might think from this that it would be a neat idea to give people new names when they are baptized. But we don't need to do that, because that has already happened. Your own baptism was a naming ceremony: you were baptized "in[to] the name of the Father and of the Son and of the Holy Spirit" (Matt. 28:19). That naming ceremony no more changed your heart than did the name you were given at birth. But like the registration of your family name, this new name expresses who you really are as a Christian believer; it is a constant reminder to you of the family to which you belong and what it means to be part of it. Our baptism is meant to be a daily reminder of this—for the rest of our lives. That is why the New Testament has so much to say about its ongoing significance for believers.

The second incident also happened in the Far East. With three other men I was invited by the owner of a famous hotel to have dinner with him—the kind of hotel where the suites would cost you more than $15,000—*per night!* The owner wore one of those watches you see advertised but learn online that you could never afford! He was a very gracious host. His splendid European chef appeared in the private dining room to explain the menu he had chosen for us—including "zee special white truffle" on the soup, and a steak that almost melted in the mouth. The company was enjoyable, and the food was exquisite. The whole experience was memorable, not least the way, when we arrived, it seemed that a pathway through the hotel had been created by the staff—we were surely very important people to the owner!

But the truth is, all the evening gave me was a story to tell you. For all the kindness of our host, he inhabited a different social world than I. The watch he was wearing was probably worth more than the house I live in. I could never afford to spend a night in his hotel. It was very thoughtful of him to invite me to come, and I said so as his driver opened the door of his magnificent limousine to take him home! It was a little like a holiday abroad—for a night!

But I tell you the story to make a point. An "experience" though it was, I would readily swap it for the opportunity to sit down at a table and have something to eat and drink with the Lord Jesus. And the wonderful truth is that I can and do, every time we share the Lord's Supper. That is why many churches refer to it as the *Communion* service. It isn't because we "*take* Communion." It is because we *experience* communion with Christ. For that is what Communion is. The most expensive meal we ever have on earth cannot hope to compare to that.

This is what *Truth We Can Touch* will help you to see more clearly. It will help you to understand how your baptism can be a lifelong help to living for Christ. And it will show you that the Lord's Supper isn't so much something we do but the way Christ enables us to enjoy his presence. In it he says to us, "Behold, I stand at the door and knock. If anyone hears my voice and opens the door, I will come in to him and eat with him, and he with me" (Rev. 3:20). When that happens, we discover—as the two disciples on the road from Jerusalem to Emmaus also did (Luke 24:28–31)—that when he comes and is present at the table, he becomes the host and gives us his little love gifts of bread and wine—visible, tangible, tasteable expressions of his dying love for us. And we recognize his presence with us. What meal could possibly mean more to us?

It is because the Lord Jesus Christ gave baptism and the Lord's Supper to us in order to bless us that I especially appreciate Tim Chester's whole approach in *Truth We Can Touch*. He has his own convictions about the various theological and practical controversies that have surrounded these gifts of Christ. But his goal here is not to satisfy our sometimes-warped desire to have the "right" positions on these sad disagreements. He has chosen a better way: to show us how to appreciate, rightly use, and enjoy the gifts themselves, because through them we come increasingly to know, trust, love, and enjoy their giver. This, after all, is why our Lord Jesus gave them to us.

So I, for one, believe that what Tim Chester writes here can only bring more and more blessing to us as individuals and as churches, and that it will enhance our appreciation and enjoyment of the privileges we receive as Christian believers. And in encouraging you now to turn over the page and read on, I feel sure that if you want to grow in grace and in the knowledge of our Lord Jesus Christ, you will not be disappointed.

Sinclair B. Ferguson

INTRODUCTION

Why Water, Bread, and Wine?

Let me invite you to try three thought experiments with me.

Thought Experiment 1

Imagine your church stopped celebrating Communion. Nothing is announced. It just stops happening. Everything else goes on as before. You gather each Sunday to sing God's praises and hear his word. You meet midweek to study the Bible and pray together. You get involved in evangelistic initiatives and serve your local community. But Communion doesn't happen.

How long do you think it would be before you noticed? What difference would it make to your life? To your life together as a church? Would you miss it?

All good experiments have a control sample, and this one is no exception. As a control, imagine what would happen if your church stopped singing. Again, no announcement is made. But next Sunday there's no music group or organist; there are no hymn numbers or songs on the screen. The Bible is read, prayers are offered, a sermon is preached. But there's no music.

Same questions: How long do you think it would be before you noticed? What difference would it make to your life? To your life together as a church? Would you miss it?

Here's my hunch. In the no-singing scenario there would be an uproar after the very first meeting. A group of people would surround the leaders demanding to know what was going on. People would be pointing in open Bibles to Colossians 3:16. Veiled threats would be made. But what about the no-Communion scenario? I fear that many Christians could skip Communion without missing very much, and perhaps without even noticing for some time.

Thought Experiment 2

Our second thought experiment takes the form of a question: When did you last point someone to his or her baptism?

Let's assume you're involved in discipling and pastoring other people in your church. Perhaps you read the Bible regularly with someone. Perhaps you're part of a prayer partnership. Perhaps you're a youth group leader. In these kinds of contexts, how often do you point people to their baptism?

I ask the question because it's something Paul does often in his letters. Check out 1 Corinthians 12:12–14, Galatians 3:26–29, and Colossians 2:11–12 if you don't believe me. Peter does the same thing in 1 Peter 3:18–22. For the apostles, baptism was not simply an event that took place back in the day. For them it shaped the whole Christian life. Christians were baptized people living a baptized life. So why don't we live like this? Lewis Allen writes:

> Where did we go wrong, that we preachers have so undervalued the Lord's Supper and baptism? A glance around evangelical churches shows that the sacraments are the

church's Cinderellas—tolerated, patronized, and even put to work, but little loved and even less gloried in. We love to celebrate a baptism and share the joy of grace in a person's life; but do we teach the saints to live in the light of their baptism, and to draw strength from the fact that they bear the name of the Trinity? And are our Supper services more obligation than celebration, something we would feel embarrassed to leave out of our worship, rather than something we love to share together?[1]

Thought Experiment 3

Some of you might find our third thought experiment a bit tougher. This might hurt. This time round you can do the thought experiment for real if you want. Go online and find a picture of a cute-looking kitten. Apparently, half the Internet is made up of cat photos, so this shouldn't be too hard. Print it out and then pin it on a dart board. You can probably see what's coming. Now throw darts at it. Me-OW!

Those of you of a certain callous disposition might relish this idea. But what about the rest of us? Most of us instinctively hesitate to throw the dart. But why? It is, after all, just a piece of paper. No actual kittens were harmed in the making of this exercise. What's going on? It's clear why we would be reluctant to hurt an actual kitten, but why do we find it hard to harm a photo of a kitten?

It's not just kitten photos that have this effect.

It was hot and the electricity in the hotel had failed. That meant no fan, no water pump, no flushing toilets. I was in the middle of nowhere. I had nothing to do until the next day, and there was nothing to distract me. I lay on the bed in my T-shirt trying not to move and dreaming of frosty November mornings

---

1. Lewis Allen, *The Preacher's Catechism* (Wheaton, IL: Crossway, 2018), 180.

back in England. What brought comfort was pulling out a rather battered photo of my wife and daughters. Of course, it didn't make them present in the room, at least not physically present. (I wouldn't have wished that on them.) It was only a piece of paper. But somehow it brought them close. It made them feel a bit more alive to me.

Or imagine someone burning the Stars and Stripes or the Union Jack or the flag of whatever happens to be your home country. We've all seen pictures of a crowd of people on the television news, cheering as the flag of their enemy burns. Why is this act so emotive? After all, it's just a piece of cloth. Yet a burning flag is powerful. For the crowd it provides a focus for protest and a release of frustration. For others it provokes anger; they may feel somehow personally violated.

In one sense symbols and signs have no intrinsic value: a photo is just a piece of paper; a flag is just a piece of cloth. But intuitively we know they are much more than the materials from which they're made. We invest them with meaning, and that meaning is, well, meaningful—they are full of meaning. There can be a real and strong link between signs and the things they signify.

Baptism is "just" water. Communion is "just" bread and wine. But there is no "just" about it. The sacraments are full of meaning. They have power.

In the local church in which I grew up, young potential preachers were given an opportunity to speak a word at the Communion service, a short introduction to what was about to take place. Thus it was that at the age of eighteen I first "preached" to a congregation. And I can remember what I said. I spoke on 1 Corinthians 10:17: "Because there is one bread, we who are many are one body, for we all partake of the one bread." My main point was that "something happens" at Communion. I'm not sure it was articulated with any more clarity than that. But I was theologically aware enough to realize what I was saying might be controversial. I had picked up that most of the people in my church saw Communion primarily, perhaps only, as a memorial of a past event. We looked back to what God had done in Christ two thousand years ago, but we didn't expect God to do anything today as we shared bread and wine. So I realized some people might disagree with what I said. Still, I was a young, arrogant teenager, so I plowed on regardless. As it happens, nothing was said afterward, and I was not excommunicated as a heretic. Perhaps being the pastor's son helped.

Often since, I have reflected on that early theological "hunch." I've not grown out of it. Quite the opposite. My estimation of the sacraments has only grown over the years, even though within evangelical circles they're rarely discussed. Indeed, there are those who seem keen to play down the significance of the sacraments. When baptism and Communion are talked about, we're more often told what they do *not* mean than what they do mean.

Why is this? Let me suggest a couple of possible reasons.

Yesterday's Battles

First, we are still fighting the debates of the sixteenth and nineteenth centuries.

The Reformation in the sixteenth century was a great return to the biblical gospel. To the fore were two big issues. First, there was a rediscovery of justification by faith alone—we are saved entirely by trusting in Christ's finished work rather than through a process of moral transformation. Second, there was a reaffirmation that our faith is built on the authority of Scripture alone—the Bible and not church tradition is our supreme authority.

But the sacraments were a close third. The Reformers rejected the idea that the sacraments are effective irrespective of the faith of those involved, and therefore they rejected the idea that babies are born again simply by being baptized. They also rejected the idea that Christ is offered as a sacrifice to God afresh in the "mass," along with the claim that the bread and wine become the physical body and blood of Christ.

These issues resurfaced in the nineteenth century with the emergence of the Oxford Movement, a movement that sought to bring about a renewal of Catholic ideas in the Church of England. The Oxford Movement gained a lot of traction at the time, and evangelicals felt embattled. As a result, the sacraments can feel like dangerous ground. Like a field full of land mines, they become surrounded by warnings signs. "Don't go there" is the message.

Today's Mindset

Second, we are children of modernity. Our modern world is the product of the Enlightenment, the intellectual movement of the eighteenth and nineteenth centuries that placed human reason front and center. The starting gun of the Enlightenment is usually recognized to be René Descartes's claim "I think, therefore I am." What is significant for our purpose is not what Descartes concluded (we'll take for granted that Descartes existed), but the manner in which he arrived at that conclusion. Descartes deliberately excluded any input from the world around him. His experience of the world could, he feared, be an illusion. He needed a basis for truth that transcended what he saw and heard and touched (or what he feared he might only be imagining he saw and heard and touched). So he made human reason the ultimate basis for knowledge. Ever since Descartes, modern people have assumed truth operates in the realm of the mind. Our essential selves reside in our thoughts, memories, and hopes. The world around us—including our own bodies—is separate from our real selves.

This worldview both collides with and, in part, fits with evangelical religion. The collision is obvious. In the modern worldview, human reason trumps divine revelation. And so the Enlightenment has seen a series of hotly contested debates and supposed contradictions between reason and revelation—debates about the historicity of the resurrection and the virgin birth, evolution and creation, the meaning of the incarnation, the authority of Scripture, the nature of miracles, the reality of prayer, and so on.

What is less often recognized is that in some key ways modernity has proved a good fit for evangelical religion, in particular its emphasis on truth residing in the mind. For evangelicalism is a religion of the word. We preach the truth of God's word to convert people by persuading them to accept the claims of the gospel and put their trust in Christ. The action, as it were, takes place in people's minds. All well and good.

But this leaves us uncertain about the sacraments. We're not sure what they're for or what we're supposed to do with them. In the sacraments, truth is embodied in water, bread, and wine—in physical substances. And in the sacraments this truth is appropriated by our bodies—we get wet, we eat bread, we drink wine.

So one of the issues I want to explore in this book is the physicality of the sacraments. Why all this water? Why bread and wine? Sometime it feels like we would have been happier if Jesus had said, "*Say* this in remembrance of me," or "*Think* this in remembrance of me." That would have fit so much better into our Western, modernistic worldview—it would have made Descartes happy. But, no, Jesus said, "*Do* this in remembrance of me" (1 Cor. 11:24). And then he handed us bread and wine and water.

There can sometimes be a sense that the sacraments are something of an embarrassment to modern evangelicals. We're not sure what to make of them and what to do with them. To be sure, in Baptist churches baptism is often relished as a great celebration of the triumph of conversion. I hope it is God's regenerating power that is being lauded, though sometimes I fear the focus is on the church's evangelistic success. But it remains unclear whether baptism serves any further purpose in a person's life.

Rediscovering the Sacraments

I have sometimes wondered if I was moving away from my heritage in the Reformers and Puritans. Perhaps I was becoming (whisper it quietly) "a bit sacramental." But what I have found as I've studied the theology of the Reformation and its successors is a much richer, fuller understanding of the sacraments. Far from drifting away from my Reformed roots, I was actually returning to them. Robert Letham writes, "Nothing presents a starker contrast between our own day and the Reformation than the current neglect of the Lord's Supper. . . . Today, the communion hardly features as a matter of significance. It is seen as an optional extra."[2]

But I've also noticed, particularly as my interest in the sacraments has attuned me to the issue over the past ten years or so, that on the ground, as it were, many, many Christians value the sacraments highly. They find them to be a great source of comfort. It's this instinct I want to articulate and encourage.

One issue I'm ignoring is whether infants should be baptized (the paedobaptist position) or just those professing faith

---

2. Robert Letham, *The Lord's Supper: Eternal Word in Broken Bread* (Phillipsburg, NJ: P&R, 2001), 1.

(the credobaptist or Baptist position). It's clearly an important issue. But it's not the focus of my concern in this book. Indeed, I fear it often distracts us from a serious consideration of the wider significance of the sacraments to our daily lives as Christians and congregations. I realize that this may frustrate some people, but there are plenty of other books to which you can turn to explore those debates.

There is, however, one aspect of the debate that we cannot completely ignore, and that is the question of what baptism signifies. Paedobaptists emphasize the way baptism signifies the work or promises of God. But evangelical and Reformed paedobaptists also emphasis the need to respond to these promises with faith. Meanwhile many credobaptists emphasize the way baptism signifies our response of faith. But Reformed credobaptists also emphasize God's initiative in salvation so that baptism is much more than simply a sign of an individual's decision to follow Christ. So all evangelicals agree that faith is vital—even when they disagree about the sequence of baptism and faith. Yet I want to argue that our *primary* focus when we think about baptism should not be on our faith, but on the object of our faith—Jesus Christ. I think this is consistent with both an evangelical paedobaptist position and a Reformed credobaptist position. If you've grown up in the kind of Baptist circles where the focus is all on the commitment we make in baptism, then this emphasis may initially appear unfamiliar. But I hope you will see that, while it is true that baptism is in part a sign of faith, first and foremost it points us away from ourselves to the promises of God and the work of Christ. As we recognize this, we will discover how God uses baptism and Communion to strengthen our faith and reassure our hearts.

Above all, I want us to learn to appreciate baptism and Communion. Christ gave them to us to nurture our faith. I want us to understand how we can approach them so they do this. They do more than simply work on our minds to teach or remind us—otherwise Christ would merely have given words to say or truth to remember. Working out what the "more than" involves is the theme of this book. What is the added value of *physical* acts? Or, to put it another way, why water, bread, and wine? Why not just thoughts and words? I don't believe the water, bread, and wine work like medicine or magic. They "work" as we respond to them in faith. But that means the more we understand and appreciate what they signify, the more benefit they will bring, and the more we will value them. So, what does it mean to live a baptized life and be a baptized body? How should we receive Communion?

I

ENACTED PROMISE

What's a human being? What are human beings like? There are many ways in which we could answer that question.

- We are creatures dependent on our Creator.
- We are social beings made to live in community.
- We are made in the image of God for a relationship with him.
- We have a tremendous capacity for creativity and kindness.

But there is one other answer that we cannot ignore: we are wicked people whose hearts are inclined to evil.

Of course, we do not like to think of ourselves as evil people. It is not a very inspiring thought! We routinely minimize or excuse our wickedness. But this is who we are. And perhaps in our more honest moments we recognize it. Certainly the evidence of history piles up in support of this conclusion.

More significantly, this is the verdict of God. Genesis 6:5 says, "The LORD saw that the wickedness of man was great in the earth, and that every intention of the thoughts of his heart was only evil continually." The indictment could not be more complete: *every* intention, *only* evil, *all* the time.

What is God's response? Judgment. Why do Christians keep going on about sin? What is this morbid fascination with failure? The answer is that we cannot ignore God's judgment in favor of some happy thoughts because judgment is the biggest problem we all face. A just and holy God will respond to evil with judgment. He must do so—otherwise he would cease to be just and holy. And God cannot do that.

God's judgment is what happens in the story of Noah in Genesis 6–9. This judgment takes the form of water. God sends a flood to wipe out humanity. In effect God *un*-creates his world. Back at creation, God separated the waters to create dry land. He brought order from chaos. At the flood the waters recombine to cover the land, and chaos returns—a chaos that drowns humanity in watery judgment.

Saved through the Judgment Symbolized by Water

But God is also gracious, and in his grace he creates a new future for humanity. He saves Noah and his family. In the ark, Noah comes through the waters of judgment. Then God sends a wind. In Hebrew the word translated "wind" is the same word used for "Spirit." Just as the Spirit hovered over the waters at creation (Gen. 1:2), so God again sends his Spirit-wind, separating the waters to create dry land. In a sense, humanity and the earth in which we live are reborn or re-created out of judgment.

The waters of that ancient flood become a symbol of God's judgment throughout the Bible story.

Later God rescues his people, Israel, from slavery in Egypt through Moses. The people find themselves caught between the pursuing Egyptian army and the sea. There appears to be no escape from death. But again God sends his Spirit-wind. Again

God separates the waters to create dry land. Exodus 14:21–22 says: "The LORD drove the sea back by a strong east wind all night and made the sea dry land, and the waters were divided. And the people of Israel went into the midst of the sea on dry ground, the waters being a wall to them on their right hand and on their left." Moses leads the people through the water on dry "ground" or dry "land" (it is the same word in Hebrew). God's people escape from death through water. But when the Egyptian army follows them, God again un-creates in judgment. The waters un-separate. They fold back on one another, and the Egyptians are drowned—just like humanity in the time of Noah. God judges Egypt with water and, at the same time, saves his people *through* water.

Forty years later, Joshua, the successor to Moses, brings a new generation of Israelites to the edge of the land God has promised them. Yet, between the people and the land is the Jordan River "at flood stage" (Josh. 3:15 NIV). But as soon as the people touch the river, the waters upstream pile up "in a heap" (Josh. 3:16), and, we read, "Israel passed over this Jordan on dry ground" (or "dry land") (Josh. 4:22). Joshua says, "For the LORD your God dried up the waters of the Jordan for you until you passed over, as the LORD your God did to the Red Sea, which he dried up for us until we passed over" (Josh. 4:23). God's people are again reborn into a new land through water.

Fast-forward to Jesus. Once again we find ourselves on the banks of the river Jordan. John the Baptist has been baptizing people—immersing them in water. We're told he was "proclaiming a baptism of repentance for the forgiveness of sins" (Mark 1:4). At that time baptism was what Gentiles did to join God's people. Gentiles had not been part of the nation that had passed through the waters of the Sea with Moses, nor through the waters of the river with Joshua. So they had to pass symbolically through water to join God's people—a kind of accelerated catch-up.

But now John is baptizing *Jews*. These Jews recognize that, in effect, they are like Gentiles. They are wicked. They face God's judgment. They need forgiveness. They need to be reborn by the Spirit through water. They need to reenter a renewed land.

Then Jesus steps forward from the crowd. Here is the Son of God, the Word made flesh. He is perfect, sinless, spotless, righteous. He doesn't need to repent. He doesn't need forgiveness. He doesn't need to be reborn.

And yet he steps into the water—the water that symbolizes our sin and our judgment. Jesus steps into our mess, our wickedness, our judgment. He identifies with us. It's a dramatic expression of intent. Jesus is symbolically engulfed by the waters of judgment. All those stories from the Old Testament were setting us up to understand *this* moment. In his baptism, Jesus identifies with his people and expresses his intent to take the judgment we deserve. Jesus is declaring, "I'm with you." It is the sign of the incarnation—Jesus has become one with humanity.

Then we read: "And when [Jesus] came up out of the water, immediately he saw the heavens being torn open and the Spirit descending on him like a dove. And a voice came from heaven, 'You are my beloved Son; with you I am well pleased'" (Mark 1:10–11). Notice that once again the Spirit is involved. God the Spirit descends on God the Son, and God the Father speaks from heaven. Mark emphasizes that this took place "immediately" after Jesus came out of the water. The Holy Trinity is united in affirming this act of identification through baptism. This is the plan.

The Father says, "You are my beloved Son; with you I am well pleased." What is Jesus doing when the Father speaks these words? He is dripping with water—water that symbolizes judgment. He's identifying with sinners as the drops run down his face. Having passed through the waters of judgment, he receives the verdict: "You are my Son. I love you. You give me pleasure."

There's a second reference to baptism in Mark's Gospel. Two of the disciples ask to sit on the left and right sides of Jesus when Jesus reigns as King. Jesus replies, "'Are you able to drink the cup that I drink, or to be baptized with the baptism with which I am baptized?" (Mark 10:38). He's talking about the cross. At the cross, Jesus will drain the cup of God's wrath on our behalf. The cup of cursing is filled with our sin and will be drained by Christ at the cross so that the cup of blessing is filled with Christ's merits and drunk by us at the Lord's Supper. And Jesus will be baptized with God's judgment on our behalf. In the Jordan River, Jesus was symbolically baptized into our sins. On the cross he is actually and really baptized into our sins. He is immersed in our sin—completely covered. He dies and is buried. He bears our judgment in full.

And on the third day, he rises again. He passes through judgment to give us new life.

Nearly forty years ago I, too, stood on the edge of water and then stepped in. I was baptized. Like Noah, like Moses, like Joshua, like Jesus, I passed through water.

Saved by the Promise Embodied in Baptism

This is how Peter explains what was happening in that moment:

> Long ago ... God waited patiently in the days of Noah while the ark was being built. In it only a few people, eight in all, were saved through water, and this water symbolizes baptism that now saves you also—not the removal of dirt

from the body but the pledge of a clear conscience toward God. It saves you by the resurrection of Jesus Christ. (1 Pet. 3:20–21 NIV)

Notice, first, Peter says Noah was "saved through water." "Through" can be a bit ambiguous in English. Here it doesn't mean "by." We're not saved *by* the waters of baptism. Noah certainly wasn't saved *by* the waters of the flood. Quite the opposite. He was *threatened* by the water. Instead, he was saved *from* the water *by* the ark. Peter says Noah was saved "in" or "into" the ark. So "saved through water" means kept safe as he passed through the water. Noah was kept safe by God as he passed through the waters of judgment to a new life.

Second, Peter says the story of Noah is reenacted in baptism. "This water symbolizes baptism," says verse 21 (NIV). Like Noah, in baptism we are saved through water. We pass through the water that symbolizes judgment and we emerge to a new life.

The word translated "symbolizes" implies an "antitype" or pattern. You have a prototype or a picture, and you have its fulfillment in an antitype, the reality to which the picture points. This means Peter is not simply coming up with an interesting parallel. He's not simply saying, "You know what? It's a bit like Noah." Instead, Peter is saying God has worked throughout history according to a pattern. The stories of Noah, Moses, and Joshua all took place as they did to prepare us to understand the meaning of Jesus. So it's not so much that the story of Noah is reenacted in our baptism. It's more that our baptism was *pre*-enacted in the story of Noah. Noah is the set up, and baptism is the punch line.

Third, Peter says baptism saves you. Many of us might blanch at these words. But we need to take what Peter says seriously. The beginning of verse 21 states, "This water symbolizes baptism *that now saves you*" (NIV). Baptism saves you.

What does Peter mean? He does *not* mean that those who are baptized are automatically saved regardless of their faith or their lack of faith. *Nor* does he mean the water has magical healing or cleansing properties. He specifically rejects any such notions in verse 21, where he says baptism is not "a removal of dirt from the body." It's literally "from the flesh"—a word commonly used in the New Testament to describe humanity in sin. Instead, baptism "saves you by the resurrection of Jesus Christ" (NIV).

When Peter says, "Baptism . . . now saves you," he's saying something similar to what we affirm when we say, "The gospel saves you." The gospel is God's promise. It's the promise that the death and resurrection of Jesus have dealt with the problem of sin and judgment—if we put our faith in Jesus. *Baptism is that promise in physical form.* Marcus Peter Johnson puts it this way: "Baptism is not something other than the gospel, it is the gospel in three-dimensional form, the experience and assurance of which we live for the rest of our lives."[1] Baptism is God's promise that we have been saved "through the resurrection of Jesus Christ" (v. 21).

Think of it like this. The Puritan Stephen Charnock says, "The gospel sacraments seal the gospel promises, as a ring confirms the covenant of marriage."[2] In a wedding both the bride and groom say, "With this ring I thee wed." The exchange of rings is instrumental in making the marriage. Just as Peter says baptism saves you, so we might say the exchanges of rings makes you married.

---

1. Marcus Peter Johnson, *One with Christ: An Evangelical Theology of Salvation* (Wheaton, IL: Crossway, 2013), 231.

2. Stephen Charnock, "A Discourse upon the Goodness of God," in *The Complete Works of Stephen Charnock*, vol. 2 (Edinburgh: James Nichol, 1864), 342–43, modernized.

Does this mean the act of handing over a ring makes someone married? If I slip a ring on your finger before you realize what's going on, are we married? No, clearly not. Does the act of being baptized in and of itself make someone a Christian? If someone falls into the baptistery (it happens) or gets splashed with water from the font, is he or she thereby united to Christ? No, clearly not. The exchanging of rings makes a marriage only in the context of a wedding ceremony in which vows are freely made. Likewise, baptism through water makes someone a Christian only when someone responds with faith to the promises embodied in baptism, and only in the context of a baptismal ceremony conducted by the church. In that wider context we can appropriately say that baptism saves you, especially if you remember that being baptized was the way people responded to the gospel in the apostolic era.

Today, people are often invited to come to the front or repeat the sinner's prayer. In this sense, saying that someone is saved by baptism is akin to saying someone is saved by praying the sinner's prayer. Merely pronouncing the words in the sinner's prayer does not automatically save you. But when it is said with sincerity in response to a gospel presentation, then this kind of language makes sense. One might only wish that the New Testament mode of response (baptism) were being used instead.

One more point needs to be made from our wedding analogy. Suppose the moment in the wedding ceremony comes for the exchange of rings and the best man realizes he's left them at home on the mantelpiece. Is the marriage off? Is the wedding invalid? No. The couple can still be married. You can be married without a ring. But something is missing, something that will need to be rectified at a later date. The rings are a sign of a couple's marriage. They're important as reminders to the couple of their vows they've received and as a declaration to the world of their new loyalties. If a true believer is not baptized at the time of conversion, does this invalidate the person's union with Christ? No. The believer is still converted and still heaven-bound—just think of the penitent thief on the cross. Nevertheless, something is missing, something that ought to be rectified as soon as possible. Baptism is an important reminder of Christ's covenant commitment to us and a declaration of our new loyalty to him and his people.

On the day of Pentecost the Spirit-wind of God again blew over God's people, this time to fill them with courage and power. The apostle Peter proclaimed the death and resurrection of Jesus. His hearers were "cut to the heart" and said, "What shall we do?" (Acts 2:37). Peter replied: "Repent and be baptized every one of you in the name of Jesus Christ for the forgiveness of your sins, and you will receive the gift of the Holy Spirit. For the promise is for you and for your children and for all who are far off, everyone whom the Lord our God calls to himself" (Acts 2:38–39). What must we do, according to Peter? We must be baptized. We must go through the waters—the waters that symbolize judgment and sin. As we do so, we're acknowledging God's verdict on humanity. We're saying, "Yes, I am wicked and I do deserve judgment." But more importantly, we're identifying with Jesus. Just as Jesus identified with *us* in *his* baptism, so we identify we *him* in *our* baptism. We unite ourselves to Jesus. So his death is our death, and his new life is our new life.

So my baptism points me away from myself and toward the baptism with which Jesus was baptized. I'm saved by the cross-baptism of Jesus, his baptism into suffering and death on my behalf. My baptism points me to that baptism: *the* baptism of the cross. It is a sign and seal of what the baptism of Jesus brings to me. You are baptized "*in* the name of Jesus *for* the forgiveness of your sins," says Peter (Acts 2:38). Baptism points me to my union with Christ. This is how New Testament believers thought of themselves, as those who are "in Christ." Just as future generations of Israel lived as free people in the promised land because the first generation had passed through the waters of the sea and the river, so we live as free people with an inheritance in the new creation because Jesus (our progenitor) passed through the judgment of death.

Pledges, Seals, Witnesses, Signs, and Bonds

Peter says baptism is "the pledge of a clear conscience toward God" (1 Pet. 3:21 NIV). It's not obvious whether he means our pledge to God or God's pledge to us. The word translated "pledge" appears only here in the New Testament and only in Daniel 4:17 in the Septuagint, the Greek translation of the Old Testament. The verb to which it is related can mean "request." So some people take this to mean that in baptism we make a request that God will give us a clear conscience. But the normal meaning of the noun is "pledge." In Daniel 4:17 it means a "decree." Some commentators assume *we* make the pledge (or request), presumably because it is made "to God." But it could be that the "clear conscience" is "to" or "before" God. So Peter could be saying that it is God who makes the pledge that we now have a clear conscience toward him. Baptism is God's decree that we are righteous in his sight. After all, Peter has just said, "For Christ also suffered once for sins, the righteous for the unrighteous, that he might bring us to God" (1 Pet. 3:18). In Romans 4:11, Paul describes circumcision as a "sign," "as a seal of the righteousness that [Abraham] had by faith while he was still uncircumcised." In the same way, baptism is a sign and seal of God's promise to us of salvation in Christ.

The word "sacrament" comes from the Latin word *sacramentum*. It was used in two ways at the time. First, it described the oath taken by soldiers in the Roman army. It was a sacred pledge of allegiance. Second, if you were suing someone in Roman civil law, then both parties deposited the contested amount into a common fund. At the end of the case, it was winner takes all. But until that moment, the deposited money was *sacramentum* or, as we might say today, "sacrosanct." In this sense *sacramentum* implied that the water, bread, and wine were set apart from their ordinary use to represent God's promise or pledge to us in the gospel, along with our corresponding response of commitment.

Matters were confused by the fact that *sacramentum* was also used to translate the Greek word for "mystery" (*mystērion*). This is used in the New Testament to refer to the revelation of Christ in the gospel (Col. 1:27; 2:2; 1 Tim. 3:16) and the relationship of Christ to the church. But *mystērion* is never used of the sacraments in the New Testament. The problem was that the association with the word "mystery" meant the sacraments were confused with the religious practices of Roman "mystery religions," which were thought to convey magical powers on the worshipers. So in medieval theology the sacraments were commonly seen as objects with inherent spiritual power.

To avoid these mistaken associations some churches have preferred the term "ordinances" to describe baptism and Communion, since they are activities "ordained" by Christ. The problem with this term, though, is that it doesn't distinguish baptism and Communion from the other activities Christ has ordained (like preaching and prayer). Baptism and Communion have distinctive roles as expressions of joining and belonging to the church. Plus, their physicality sets them apart and requires us to think about them in a distinctive way.

This language of pledge, seal, sign, and witness reflects the language used in the creeds of Reformation churches. The

French or Gallic Confession of Faith, a statement drafted by Calvin and adopted by the French Reformed churches in 1559, affirms that the sacraments serve as "pledges and seals of the grace of God, and by this means aid and comfort our faith because of the infirmity which is in us" (§34). It describes baptism as "a pledge of our adoption" and "a lasting witness that Jesus Christ will always be our justification and sanctification" (§35). Likewise the Supper is "a witness of the union which we have with Christ" (§36). The Belgic Confession (1561), one of the confessional standards of the Dutch Reformed churches, also speaks of the sacraments as "seals" and "pledges" "to nourish and strengthen our faith" (§33). The Thirty-Nine Articles of 1563, the historic confession of the Anglican Church, say the sacraments are not only "badges" or "tokens" of our profession but also "sure witnesses, and effectual signs of grace, and God's good will towards us," which are given to "strengthen and confirm our faith in him" (Art. 25). The Westminster Confession was written by English-speaking Puritans in the 1640s and became the main statement of faith of Presbyterians and, in adapted forms, Congregationalists and Reformed Baptists. It speaks of the sacraments as "seals of the covenant of grace" (27.1). The Lord's Supper is "a bond and pledge of [believers'] communion with [Christ], and with each other, as members of his mystical body" (29.1).

Think of a contract. Think perhaps of an employment contract or a memorandum of sale or an IOU. What you hold in your hand is a sheet of paper with a series of commitments written on it. This is what the gospel is: a series of promises expressed in words. God promises forgiveness, acquittal, adoption, preservation, resurrection, and glory. The sacraments are like the signature at the bottom of the contract. In the past, agreements weren't signed; they were sealed with a wax impression. So the Reformers spoke of the sacraments as seals. But today a signature is our normal way of confirming commitments. The covenant promises God makes to us in the gospel are signed and sealed with water, bread, and wine. The signature doesn't add any new content to the promises; nor does it enact them. But it does seal and confirm those promises. Without a signed contract you might still have reason to be optimistic that someone would fulfill his or her promises, but a signature gives you much greater confidence. You have something you can point to, a commitment you can hold in your hand. And God has graciously given us baptism and Communion to give us greater confidence in his promises.

In the preaching of the gospel, God gives us the promise of the forgiveness in a form we can hear. That's the form that comes with clarity because it comes in the form of words. Without those words we wouldn't understand the gospel. But in the sacraments God also gives us the promise of forgiveness in a form we can see, touch, and even taste. The water, bread, and wine are added as confirmations of the reality of the promise. All our senses are thus engaged so that our frail faith might be nurtured. Jesus describes the wine as the "blood of the new covenant." A covenant is a relationship-forming promise. Here is God's promise in physical form so we can see it as well as hear it, taste it as well as read it.

Truth We Can Touch

This means my baptism preaches the gospel to me. And baptism does so in a very important way. It is an external act and a physical reality. It's truth we can touch. So baptism creates a very powerful promise.

Today you might feel forgiven. You might feel like a new person. You may feel loved by God. But what about tomorrow? What about the day when you sin spectacularly? Or when cancer is diagnosed? Or when you're betrayed by a loved one? How will you feel then? Will you feel forgiven when you've sinned? Will you feel like a new person when cancer is eating your body? Will you feel loved when you're unloved? A hope based on our feelings or our circumstances is a hope built on a shaky foundation. It will not survive the storms of life.

But our hope is based on God's promise. We have that promise in God's word. But *God in his kindness, knowing how frail we are, knowing how battered by life we can be, has also given us his promise in water, bread, and wine.* He's done so because he loves us, and he wants us to be confident in that love. It's so important that we grasp this: baptism and Communion are God's promise in physical form.

Think how this works in a marriage. If you are married and you say to your spouse, "I love you," you give a significant reassurance of your love. But you do more than simply declare it. You also kiss, hug, and touch. The declaration of your love also takes physical form. And no husband or wife thinks that physical expression of love is redundant. Kissing and hugging add to the spoken declaration.

We would rightly be suspicious of a marriage that was all physical touching without any conversation or a marriage that was all conversation without any physical affection. In the same way, a Christianity that is all word and no sacrament or all sacrament and no word is missing something vital. Melvin Tinker explains, "For just as the physical act of embracing or kissing someone is capable of conveying forgiveness and acceptance (as in the story of the Prodigal Son—Luke 15:20), so the physical act of the giving of bread and wine conveys the forgiveness and gracious acceptance of God."[3]

---

3. Melvin Tinker, "Language, Symbols and Sacraments: Was Calvin's View of the Lord's Supper Right?," *Churchman* 112, no. 2 (1998): 145.

Some evangelicals seem suspicious of people who express a desire or need for the sacraments, as if this were an indication of spiritual weakness. And in one sense they're right—it *is* an indication of spiritual weakness, an acknowledgment that we need these vivid means of grace. But what is alarming is the presumption that we are above such needs and that a cerebral communion with Christ is sufficient. Calvin says of those who question the need for visible signs, "Nothing is more odd than for the faithful freely to do without the assistance handed down by the Lord or allow themselves to be deprived."[4]

Calvin defines a sacrament as an accommodation by God to our weakness: a sacrament is "an outward sign by which the Lord seals on our consciences the promises of his good will toward us in order to sustain the weakness of our faith."[5] God provides sacraments for "our ignorance and dullness," "our weakness," "our dull capacity," and "our dullness."[6] Or as Thomas Cranmer, the great Reforming archbishop of Canterbury, says, "Our Saviour Christ, knowing us to be, as it were, babes and weaklings in faith, has ordained signs and tokens for our senses to allure and to draw us to more strength and more constant faith in him."[7]

It's not just that we are weak; it's also that the promises of the gospel are so amazing that we struggle to believe them. The Dutch Reformed minister Gerard Wisse says this:

> The promise of God in Christ Jesus is of such extraordinary magnitude that it seems almost impossible that it also

---

4. John Calvin, *A Harmony of the Gospels: Matthew, Mark and Luke and the Epistles of James and Jude*, ed. Thomas F. Torrance and David W. Torrance, trans. A. W. Morrison (Edinburgh: Saint Andrew Press, 1972), 138.

5. John Calvin, *Institutes of the Christian Religion*, ed. John T. McNeill, trans. Ford Lewis Battles, Library of Christian Classics 20–21 (Philadelphia: Westminster, 1960), 4.14.1.

6. Calvin, *Institutes*, 4.14.3, 6.

7. Thomas Cranmer, "Defence of the True and Catholic Doctrine of the Sacrament, 1550," in *The Work of Thomas Cranmer*, ed. G. E. Duffield, The Courtenay Library of Reformation Classics 2 (Appleford: Sutton Courtenay, 1964), 71–72, modernized.

applies to someone like me. Therefore the Lord, by means of His Supper, stamps the seal of confirmation upon this promise. . . . God, so to speak, places the ring of spiritual betrothal on our finger.[8]

Likewise, the Puritan Richard Vines says, "So if doubts arise concerning the reality of God and the sureness of this covenant that speaks of so much grace and mercy, we look upon and take hold of this seal of blood [in the cup of Communion], and are thereby settled and therein acquiesce."[9]

The Belgic Confession of 1516 states that the sacraments are added or "joined" to "the Word of the gospel, the better to present to our senses, both that which [God] signifies to us by his Word, and that which he works inwardly in our hearts, thereby assuring and confirming in us the salvation which he imparts to us" (§33). The grace of faith, says the Westminster Confession, is "ordinarily wrought by the ministry of the Word" but also "increased and strengthened" by the sacraments (14.1).

So word and sacrament work together. Augustine says the sacraments are "a kind of visible word" of God,[10] while the Puritan Thomas Watson describes the Lord's Supper as "a visible sermon."[11] John Calvin declares, "Let it be regarded as a settled principle that the sacraments have the same office as the Word of God: to offer and set forth Christ to us, and in him

---

8. Gerard Wisse, "May I Partake of the Lord's Supper?," in Wisse, *Christ's Ministry in the Christian: The Administration of His Offices in the Believer*, trans. Bartel Elshout and William Van Voorst (Sioux Center, IA: Netherlands Reformed, 1993), 100–101, modernized.

9. Richard Vines, "The Fruit and Benefit of Worthy Receiving," in *The Puritans on the Lord's Supper*, ed. Don Kistler (Morgan, PA: Soli Deo Gloria, 1997), 120.

10. Augustine, "Tractates on the Gospel according to St. John" (80.3), in vol. 7 of *Nicene and Post-Nicene Fathers*, first series, ed. Philip Schaff (1888; Peabody, MA: Hendrickson, 1994), 344, quoted in Robert Letham, *The Lord's Supper: Eternal Word in Broken Bread* (Phillipsburg, NJ: P&R, 2001), 7.

11. Thomas Watson, "The Mystery of the Lord's Supper," in Kistler, *The Puritans on the Lord's Supper*, 127.

the treasures of heavenly grace."[12] "The content of the Word and sacrament is completely identical," says the Dutch theologian Herman Bavinck. "They only differ in the external form, in the *manner* in which they offer the *same* Christ to us. . . . In the Lord's Supper we indeed do not receive any other or any more benefits than we do in the Word, but also no fewer."[13]

In other words, the sacraments don't add anything new or different from the promises we receive in the gospel. We're not getting anything from the sacraments that we don't already have through the gospel. Indeed, the sacraments *require* the word to make clear the meaning of the promises they embody. But the sacraments do confirm those promises and reassure us that they apply to us, frail sinners though we know ourselves to be. Here's how Sinclair Ferguson puts it: "We do not get a different or a better Christ in the sacraments than we do in the Word. . . . But we may get the same Christ better, with a firmer grasp of his grace through seeing, touching, feeling, and tasting as well as hearing."[14]

Calvin goes further: "The sacraments bring *the clearest promises*," he says, "and they have this characteristic over and above the word because they represent them for us as painted in a picture from life." He adds that the sacraments attest God's "good will and love toward us *more expressly* than by word." They are *"more* evident" and *"more* certain."[15] The word communicates to our hearing. The sacraments, too, communicate to our hearing because they contain the word of promise in the words of institution (no one conducts a Communion service in complete silence). But in addition, they also communicate

---

12. Calvin, *Institutes*, 4.14.17.

13. Herman Bavinck, *Reformed Dogmatics*, vol. 4, *Holy Spirit, Church, and New Creation*, ed. John Bolt, trans. John Vriend (Grand Rapids, MI: Baker, 2008), 479, 567.

14. Sinclair B. Ferguson, *The Whole Christ* (Wheaton, IL: Crossway, 2016), 223.

15. Calvin, *Institutes*, 4.14.3, 5–6, emphasis added.

to our sight, touch, taste, and perhaps even smell in the water, bread, and wine—hence the "more" of Calvin's statements. Indeed, Calvin, who originally wrote in Latin, added a Greek word to describe the sacraments: *eikonikōs* or "icons."[16]

Consider the words Ananias spoke to Paul when they met shortly after Paul's encounter with Christ on the road to Damascus: "Rise and be baptized and wash away your sins, calling on his name" (Acts 22:16). Paul was saved by calling on Christ's name (as he explains in Rom. 10:5–13). But the promise of forgiveness took physical form for him in his baptism—so much so that, as the water covered his body, he could imagine it washing away his sins, the physical act pointing to the spiritual act that was taking place as he called on Christ's name. Over his troubled soul washed the waters of baptism. This would have acted as a deep reassurance to a man who had just been accused of persecuting the risen Christ by the risen Christ himself (Acts 22:7).

So word and sacrament go together. That doesn't mean there must always be a sermon when the Lord's Supper is administered. That's a potentially clunky application of this truth. Indeed, it can detract from the Lord's Supper as if its real meaning is left to the accompanying sermon. Instead, the principle is that there must be an explanatory context. This will involve what the Westminster Confession calls "the word of institution" (27.3). But it will also involve a wider context in which the meaning of the sacraments and the gospel they represent are taught within the congregation. The people taking Communion need to have a growing understanding of its significance. We need to teach this. And this is often absent in evangelical churches. As a result, people don't really know what they're doing when they take Communion or how they should receive it.

---

16. J. Todd Billings, *Remembrance, Communion, and Hope: Rediscovering the Gospel at the Lord's Table* (Grand Rapids, MI: Eerdmans, 2018), 18n14. See *Institutes*, 4.14.6.

A Truth beyond Feelings

I recently asked a group of people who had been baptized as believers how they felt when they were baptized. Do you know what most of them said? "Wet." That might seem like a flippant remark or an evasive joke. But it's actually a vital truth. My standing before God does not depend on how I feel inside. It depends on his promise. But how do I know that I have his promise? Because there was a day when I was wet. The promise didn't well up inside me. If that's how it came to me, then I might worry whether it was real—perhaps it was just a trick of my emotions. But instead God's promise has come to us (if you're baptized) in physical form, at a moment in history, as an external reality.

The same applies to Communion. The bread and wine are a physical embodiment of God's promise. Think of them in those terms. As the bread is handed to you, think of it as God's promise to you, his pledge, his covenant.

Here's why this is important.

There are two opposite dangers in how we view the sacraments. First, the Catholic Church says that grace is conveyed through the sacraments *ex opere operato*—"by the action of the act," irrespective of whether there is faith. This was developed to justify baptismal regeneration—the idea that people become Christians simply by being baptized. It also has the effect of making Communion the equivalent of taking a spiritual vitamin pill. What you think about a pill doesn't affect the benefit it conveys to you (at least if we ignore the placebo effect). The pill strengthens your health whether you believe it will work or not. Catholic theology believes the sacraments can be like taking medicine you don't believe in. The fact that you doubt their efficacy does not stop them working.

But sin is more than sickness; it is an act of rebellion against God. And salvation is more than healing; it is reconciliation with God. Sin and salvation—and therefore also the sacraments—are relational realities. The sacraments have value only in the context of a relationship with God in Christ. In other words, the sacraments benefit us when we have faith.

But there is an opposite danger, and this is a danger to which evangelicals are often prone. It is the danger of linking the efficacy of Communion to the way I feel about it: if I am moved, then it's effective; if I am unmoved, then it's ineffective. So, what makes it effective is my experience. What makes it effective is me! In this case, the Lord's Supper ceases to be a divine act and becomes a human act, and its power is human power.

We live in a culture where everything is about response and feeling. The validity of a truth or an action is linked to the way it makes me feel. And our contemporary evangelical culture is deeply imbued with this subjectivism. So we need to understand that the gospel is entirely outside us. The gospel is not my response. The gospel describes not my response but that to which I respond. Leonard Vander Zee comments:

> Ask most any Protestant about the meaning of the Supper, and you will hear the word *remembrance*. The problem is that a too-simplistic understanding of the Lord's command has limited the meaning of the sacrament in the minds of many to the recollection of a long-ago historical event. It tends to place the weight of the sacramental meaning in the minds, heart and faith of the participants, as he or she struggles to remember, with faith and gratitude, what the Lord did for them on the cross.[17]

---

17. Leonard J. Vander Zee, *Christ, Baptism and the Lord's Supper: Recovering the Sacraments for Evangelical Worship* (Downers Grove, IL: InterVarsity Press, 2004), 210.

This is why it is helpful to think of the sacraments as embodied promises. Their validity and power lie in the one who makes the promises. The water, bread, and wine are objective realities outside us *that embody the objective nature of the gospel promise.*

Consider the parallel with the word of God. Conversion and growth take place as someone responds to the preached word with faith. But a lack of faith does not invalidate the preaching. The word that is preached is still true, still powerful, still divine. In the same way, God's presence is felt and his promise received only when someone responds to the sacramental word with faith. But a lack of faith does not invalidate the sacrament. The meaning does not reside in my response any more than the meaning of the preached word lies in the reader's response. Thomas Cranmer put it like this:

> Christ is present in his sacraments, just as he is present in his word when he works mightily through it in the hearts of the hearers. By this we do not mean that Christ is physically present in the voice or sound of the speaker (whose sound perishes as soon as the words are spoken). Instead, by this we mean that Christ works through his word, using the voice of the speaker, as his instrument. In the same way, he also uses his sacraments, by which he works, and therefore can be said to be present in them.[18]

So it is true that baptism and Communion are effective only when we respond with faith. They are just like the *word* of God in that respect. Merely hearing a sermon doesn't save you—you need to have faith in Christ. Merely being baptized or receiving Communion doesn't save you—you need to have faith in

---

18. Thomas Cranmer, "Answer to Gardiner," in *The Works of Thomas Cranmer*, vol. 1, *On the Sacrament of the Lord's Supper*, ed. John Edmund Cox (Cambridge: Parker Society, 1844), 11, modernized.

Christ. But this does not mean that the meaning or power of baptism and Communion lies in our response—any more than the meaning of God's word lies in our response. My response matters, but it does not make the word, the water, the bread, the wine meaningful. Their meaning derives from the gospel. They are all objective declarations of God's promise to us. They derive their significance and value from Christ. So they do not come from faith. They come for faith—to create and strengthen faith.

The person who sits through a sermon deconstructing the words of the preacher or adding up the hymn numbers (as I used to do as a child) derives no benefit from the sermon. In the same way, the person who receives Communion at a special midnight Communion on Christmas Eve after an evening in a local bar without any thought of Christ (as my friends would do) derives no benefit from doing so. Indeed, in both cases, their response (or, rather, their lack of it) confirms God's judgments against their unbelief. But children of God who hear the word and receive the sacraments with faith find their faith strengthened.

Think how helpful that is. You may be full of doubt or guilt or just spiritual numbness. And here is God's promise. You hold it in your hands. You put it to your lips. This is God's kindness to you. This is God's commitment to you. This is God's *yes* to you in Christ. The forgiveness of sin is not just something I feel. It is an objective reality that took place at the cross. And we have that promise in water, bread, and wine.

I want you to feel it. But it does not depend on your feelings. It arrives in your hands and in your mouth *from God*. What gives it its meaning is not your faith or your feeling but the death and resurrection of Jesus. And so it comes to *strengthen* faith. The sacraments are not dependent on how I feel, and *therefore because of this* they are able to *change* the way I feel. They speak reassurance to my heart. Marcus Peter Johnson explains:

> Our mental remembrance of the significance of Christ's death is not able, and is not meant, to sustain us in our fragile and compromised states, full of the perplexities, doubts, tragedies, griefs, and despair that inevitably accompany us. Only Christ is able, and is meant, to do that. The Lord's Supper is God's assurance to us that we really belong to Christ in the fulness of his saving person; that we really do share in the One who, in flesh and blood, is our justification, sanctification, and redemption.[19]

An Act You Can't Perform

The leader of the baptism service said, "We're here today because Jack has decided to be baptized to express his decision to follow Jesus." I winced. After a song, this was followed by Jack telling us why he had decided to follow Jesus and why he wanted to be baptized. What could be wrong with that? In one sense, nothing. I do not object to any of this language in itself. My problem is that it is not the place to start, and it is not what matters most.

Consider what actually occurs in a baptism. Who is active and who is passive? Imagine the scene. A young man stands in a large pool of water. Then someone says, "I baptize you in the name of the Father, the Son, and the Spirit." The young man is plunged under the water and then lifted out again. Or a baby is held in the arms of the minister, who sprinkles water on his or her forehead. Who is active and who is passive? Clearly the person being baptized is passive. This reality is reflected in the

---

19. Johnson, *One with Christ*, 240.

nature of the verb "baptize." You can use the active form—"I baptize"—only if you are the officiant. For the person being baptized, the form of the verb is passive ("I am baptized").

What do you do when you are baptized? The answer is *nothing*. It is done *to* you. It is an act you can't perform for yourself. You just stand there, and someone pours water over you or immerses you in water.

It is a picture of our salvation. What did we do to be saved? Nothing. Jesus has done it all. It was Jesus who was immersed into death and hell on your behalf. In baptism you just stand there as God pours his blessing over you and immerses you in his love.

This is really important. You are not the active agent in your baptism. Your baptism is always something done *to* you, not *by* you. This is one of the strengths of the paedobaptist position. When an infant is being baptized, there can be no suggestion that this baptism is taking place as a result of the child's merits or decision. But this truth is vital whatever the age or status of the person being baptized. Indeed, the passivity of baptism is more important for credobaptists to remember because, otherwise, credobaptists tend to emphasize the actions or decision of the person being baptized. It is true that we must respond with faith to be saved. But salvation does not start with our faith. It starts with the Father's electing love, Christ's work of redemption, and the new life the Spirit works in our hearts.

So who is active in baptism? The first answer is obvious: the person conducting the baptism. He represents the church. Baptism is an act performed by the church. The church baptizes. It is a corporate act through which we welcome people into membership.

But it gets better. After all, that is still the testimony of people. And who knows—one day they may let you down. The key reality is that *God* is active in a baptism. Jack's baptism is an embodied promise from God to Jack.

In baptism (and in Communion) there is a three-way conversation:

- God says, "I have saved you by uniting you with Christ and his people."
- The church says, "We are united in Christ and committed to one another."
- I say, "I am committed to Christ and his people."

Francis Turretin says the sacraments have "primary" and "secondary" purposes. The primary purpose is to confirm the covenant of grace and seal our union with God—and this is a purpose God fulfills through the sacraments. The secondary purpose is to be a badge of our public profession of faith.[20] We will look at the declarations that the church and the individual make in future chapters. They are important because baptism does involve a covenantal commitment. But it is *really, really* important that God's voice is first and foremost. His is the voice that should dominate. "The primary movement which the gospel sacraments embody," says John Stott, "is from God to man, not man to God."[21]

The Westminster Confession captures this balance well (28.1). It says that a person's baptism is a sign and seal of five things:

- "the covenant of grace,"
- "his ingrafting into Christ,"
- "regeneration,"
- "remission of sins,"

---

20. Francis Turretin, *Institutes of Elenctic Theology*, trans. George Musgrave Giger, ed. James T. Dennison Jr., vol. 3 (Phillipsburg, NJ: P&R, 1997), 341–42.

21. John Stott, *The Cross of Christ*, 2nd ed. (Leicester: Inter-Varsity Press, 1989), 259.

- "his giving up unto God, through Jesus Christ, to walk in the newness of life."

Only the final one of these five signs is about our response; the first four describe what God does.

The 1689 Second Baptist Confession of Faith was adapted from the Westminster Confession, and, as you would expect, it changes what the Westminster Confession says about *who* should be baptized. But it retains a similar balance when it describes what baptism *signifies* (29.1). It says baptism is a sign of

- "fellowship with [Christ] in his death and resurrection,"
- "being engrafted into him,"
- "remission of sins,"
- "giving up into God, through Jesus Christ, to live and walk in newness of life."

In many Baptist circles today the emphasis tends to be on this final sign—our commitment to God. But the 1689 confession reminds us that, historically, Reformed Baptists have placed just as much emphasis as the Westminster Confession on the way baptism points us away from ourselves to our union with Christ and the promise of forgiveness.

The same is true of the Supper: it, too, primarily embodies a movement from God to us. The Dutch Reformed minister Gerard Wisse has this to say:

> Our celebration of the Lord's Supper is not in the first place an act whereby we bear witness to *our* conversion, *our* pious frame, or *our* relationship to the Lord—even though these things may also be discussed. Rather, it is primarily *God's* act towards us, whereas our partaking is the reciprocal act. . . . As a sacrament it is a warranty—a visible sealing of the veracity of *His* promises. . . . In a sacrament the focus is in

the first place on a message which comes *from God* to us— the message of who and what the triune covenant God is and remains for His people.[22]

This idea was central to the renewal of worship and liturgy at the Reformation. In the medieval church the focus was firmly on what the people did or, rather, what the priest did on behalf of the people. A service was performed *for* God or a sacrifice was offered *to* God to earn his merit. The Reformation switched this around. When the people of God gather, it is God who is active, and it is God's voice that predominates. Nicholas Wolterstorff says, "The liturgy as the Reformers understood and practiced it consists of God acting and us responding through the work of the Spirit. . . . The liturgy is a meeting between God and God's people, a meeting in which both parties act, but in which God initiates and we respond."[23]

The word "liturgy" comes from the Greek word *leitourgia,* a combination of words meaning "work" and "people." So the Catholic Church is fond of describing the liturgy and the sacraments as "the work of the people." But, in fact, "work *for* the people" would be a better translation of *leitourgia*. In the Roman world, *leitourgia* was public work donated to the populace by a rich benefactor. In the same way, the sacraments are donated to us by our great benefactor. Corporate worship is not a work we perform for God's benefit.

Again and again the Scriptures remind us that God has no need of our sacrifices. But if God does not need sacrifices, why does he ask for them? The answer is that God *gives* them as the promise and picture of full atonement through the ultimate sacrifice, Jesus Christ. Their benefit is not for God but for the

---

22. Wisse, "May I Partake of the Lord's Supper?," 100–101, emphasis added.
23. Cited in James K. A. Smith, *You Are What You Love: The Spiritual Power of Habit* (Grand Rapids, MI: Brazos, 2016), 71.

worshiper. They were given in the Old Testament to nurture faith in the coming Lamb of God. We often remind one another that the cattle on a thousand hills belong to God when we need to raise resources for some project. But in their original context those words are actually a warning not to suppose that we do something for God in our worship.

> I will not accept a bull from your house
>   or goats from your folds.
> For every beast of the forest is mine,
>   the cattle on a thousand hills.
> I know all the birds of the hills,
>   and all that moves in the field is mine.
>
> If I were hungry, I would not tell you,
>   for the world and its fullness are mine.
> Do I eat the flesh of bulls
>   or drink the blood of goats? (Ps. 50:9–13)

Instead, worship in your church on a Sunday morning is a *gift* given to you by God to nurture your faith. Psalm 50 continues with an invitation to call on God "in the day of trouble" (v. 15). Yes, we sing our praises to him, but even our praises are given as a means by which we might teach and admonish one another (Col. 3:16; see also Eph. 5:19). Yes, we "offer to God a sacrifice of thanksgiving" (Ps. 50:14; see also v. 23), but these honor God by responding to what he has done for us.

The issue is this: *Who* does the sacraments? In this respect the views of the sacraments held by Roman Catholics and many evangelicals are actually more similar than many evangelicals realize. For they both see the sacraments as something we do for God. But baptism and Communion are not something we do for God; they are something he does for us. Communion is called the Eucharist, "a thanksgiving," because it is a gift we received passively. The goal of the sacraments is not to build God up; instead, God uses them as a means of grace to build *us* up in our faith. This is why there are only two sacraments and not the seven identified by the Catholic Church. Protestants affirm some of the other five Catholic sacraments as legitimate activities—we, too, believe in marriage and ordination, for example. But we do not see these as sacraments, and that is because they are acts we do or promises we make. What makes baptism and the Supper distinctive is that they are gifts we receive from Christ.

Why does this matter?

There was a period of his life when Martin Luther, the great Reformer, was in hiding from persecution in a castle. He spent his time translating the Bible into German. But it was a dark time. The established church had rejected him, labeling him a heretic. He struggled with doubt and discouragement. On one occasion, it is said, he threw an inkpot across the room at the devil. But another one of his strategies was this. He was often heard shouting in the grounds of the castle, *Baptizatus sum*, "I am baptized." In my imagination he stands in the courtyard of the castle in the falling snow (I don't know why it's snowing, but in my imagination it is) and shouts, "I am a baptized man." How Luther felt was up and down—mostly down. His circumstances looked bleak. But his baptism was a fact, and it embodied the promise of God.

Imagine if someone had introduced Luther's baptism with the words, "We're here today because Martin has decided to be baptized to express his decision to follow Jesus." If this is how I have been taught to understand my baptism, then Luther's words have no power against the devil, no power to sustain faith, no promise of assurance. If baptism is primarily an expression of my decision, my faith, my actions, then it is as strong as I am. And that is not very strong! In the midst of doubt, why would I not also doubt the feelings I had back at my baptism? Perhaps I was mistaken. Perhaps I got carried away with the occasion.

But if, instead, I see baptism as an act performed on me from outside, then I am not left in my introspective swamp. I have a plank on which I can climb free. Baptism is not my declaration that I am okay. It is the church's declaration that I am united to Christ by faith. And it is God's promise to save me and keep me through the death and resurrection of Jesus. Fact. It is a declaration that comes to me from outside me. Baptism and the Lord's Supper are not *primarily* signs of our subjective experience or faith or response. They are signs that point us to the gospel.

In one sense, we cannot know if we are among the elect, for we have no direct access to God's secret decrees. But we do know that all who come to Jesus are saved. God's electing choice is revealed when people put their faith in Christ. "All that the Father gives me will come to me," says Jesus in John 6:37, "and whoever comes to me I will never cast out." So our concern is not to second-guess the secret things of God's election (Deut. 29:29). Our concern is, Have I entrusted myself to Jesus? When doubts come or Satan accuses or our sin throws everything into confusion, we do not turn inward and look for signs of electing grace in the murky depths of our hearts. We turn outward to look at Christ. Baptism helps us do that. It does so not because those who are baptized are automatically saved, but because the promise of Christ is expressed in visible, tangible form in baptism. When doubts arise, we put our faith afresh in Christ, who once dripped with the water that expressed his identification with sinners. We put our faith afresh in Christ, who was submerged in judgment on our behalf at the cross. We put our faith afresh in Christ, who emerged from judgment at his resurrection. We put our faith afresh in Christ, whose death and resurrection we have enacted in our own baptism.

As a child I had a long period during which I lacked assurance. It was a dark time, since I was all too aware of what was at stake. The questions that played on my mind were: Had I repented enough? Did I have enough faith? I am not sure in what units I thought faith was measured or what the pass mark was! One Sunday my father was preaching in another church and I traveled with him (something I do not remember doing on any other occasion). He preached on the words of Jesus from John 6:37 quoted above, "Whoever comes to me I will never cast out." I can remember thinking: "I've come to Jesus and he promises not to send me away. It doesn't matter how strong my faith is; what matters is that I have put that faith in Jesus." Shortly thereafter I was baptized. Ever since, when I have been troubled by doubts, I have looked back to my baptism. It is as if my baptism captured that moment of clarity when I stopped looking at myself and looked instead to Christ.

In his "Large Catechism," Luther said: "Thus, we must regard baptism and put it to use in such a way that we may draw strength and comfort from it when our sins or conscience oppress us, and say: 'But I am baptized! And if I have been baptized, I have the promise that I shall be saved and have eternal life, both in soul and body.'"[24] Of course, wandering around shouting "I am baptized" is not enough to save you if you do not have faith in Christ. But, then, people are not going to find comfort in shouting "I am baptized" unless they have some measure of faith. When we are afraid, when we feel the weight of our sin, when we feel the power of the enemy, we can say, "I am

---

24. Martin Luther "The Large Catechism," in *The Book of Concord* (1580), ed. Robert Kolb and Timothy J. Wengert (Minneapolis: Fortress, 2000), pt. 4, §44 (462).

baptized." In other words: "I have received the promise of God. God is for me. And if God is for me, who can be against me?"

What should you do when you are filled with guilt or fear or doubt? Look to the baptism of Jesus and see him dripping with water as a sign that he identifies with you in your sin. And look to your own baptism and see yourself dripping with water as God's promise that you are forgiven in Christ. You have passed through judgment to new life with Christ.

2

ENACTED GRACE

In 2010, Neil McGregor, then the director of the British Museum, gave a series of radio talks called *A History of the World in 100 Objects*. They were later published as a hugely successful book. As the title suggests, McGregor told the story of world history using one hundred objects, all of which are part of the collection of the British Museum. I want to do something similar in this chapter. I want to tell *the history of the world in twelve meals*.

The History of the World in Twelve Meals

1. Creation and the Menu for Mankind: The Story of God's Generosity

What is the very first thing God said to humanity after he created Adam and Eve and placed them in the garden of Eden? "You may surely eat of every tree of the garden" (Gen. 2:16). God's first words are a menu—a comprehensive, hunger-satisfying, pleasure-giving menu.

One of the striking features of this is that the account of creation in Genesis was almost certainly used to counter the creation stories of the Babylonian Empire. And in the Babylonian creation story, humanity was made to provide food for the gods. But with our God, the true God, it is the other way around: God provides food for humanity. The first words humanity hears from God reveal his generosity.

Not only did God provide humanity with a meal; he also walked with humanity "in the garden in the cool of the day" (Gen. 3:8). What that quite looked like it is hard for us to know, but it is clear that God was present with humanity. Humanity was made to enjoy *a meal in the presence of God.*

2. The Fall and Another Menu:
The Story of Humanity's Sin

Despite God's generosity, humanity rejected his love and rebelled against his rule. And how did we do this? By eating (Gen. 3:1–7). We chose *an alternative menu.* God had said, "You may surely eat of every tree of the garden, but of the tree of the knowledge of good and evil you shall not eat, for in the day that you eat of it you shall surely die" (Gen. 2:16–17). God offered us a vast, rich, diverse menu—we could eat from any tree. There was just one exception to enable us to express our trust in God and obedience to his rule. But we chose to doubt God's word and reject his authority. And we did that in a meal—by eating the one forbidden fruit.

Adam and Eve immediately felt ashamed and hid from God (Gen. 3:8). And we are still hiding from him. One result of that is that our relationship with food is now fraught. We were made for a meal in the presence of God, but now God often is absent at our meals. And so many of us turn to food itself for comfort. We often look to food, whether we are comfort-eating or dieting, to provide the satisfaction or identity we were meant to find in God.

3. The Passover Meal: The Story of God's Redemption

But God in his grace did not leave us to our plight. He called Abraham and promised (at one point over a meal in Gen. 18:1–15) that through Abraham's descendants God would save a people and create a new humanity (Gen. 12:1–7). God pictured that salvation in the story of Abraham's descendants, the nation of Israel. The Israelites became slaves in Egypt. But God sent Moses to lead them to freedom. He sent a series of plagues to force the king of Egypt to let God's people go free. Those plagues came to a climax with God declaring that he would kill every firstborn son in Egypt (Ex. 11).

The problem was that the people of Israel were in the firing line just as much as the Egyptians. Israel could not claim any moral superiority. They, too, were sinners who deserved God's judgment. But God in his grace provided a way of escape. At one and the same time, it was escape from the judgment of death and from the slavery of Egypt. The Israelites had to sacrifice a lamb and daub its blood around the doors of their homes. Wherever God saw the blood, he "pass[ed] over" that house (see Ex. 12:12–13). The blood protected the family inside. God's people were redeemed from slavery through the shedding of blood.

Meanwhile, inside their homes the people ate a meal. They ate the sacrificed lamb with unleavened bread as a sign of their readiness for their journey to freedom (Ex. 12:8–11). And so this redemption was commemorated in a meal, the Passover meal. Indeed, the instructions for the Passover night included instructions to celebrate it as a meal for generations to come (Ex. 12:14–20, 24–28). This annual meal would reveal to future generations who God is, what he has done, and who they were. It would prove to be an identity-forming meal. God's redemption and what it meant to be his people were *pictured in a meal*.

4. Manna from Heaven: The Story of God's Provision

Having being redeemed from Egypt, God's people set off through the desert to the land God had promised would be theirs. One month later they were grumbling (Ex. 16:1–3). What were they grumbling about? Food. Egyptian food was better than desert food, they claimed.

What did God do? What the people deserved was judgment. The rod of judgment that fell on Egypt should have fallen on God's people. But God basically told Moses to bring the rod of judgment down on God himself (Ex. 17:6). God symbolically took the judgment they deserved and in return gave them what they did not deserve: bread from heaven (Ex. 16:4) and water from a rock (Ex. 17:6). Each morning the people gathered what they called "manna," everyone gathering "as much as he could eat" (Ex. 16:18). God's grace came in the form of a meal. Eating that bread each day told the people that it is God who truly satisfies our needs.

5. A Meal on the Mountain: The Story of God's Covenant

God led his people to Mount Sinai, and there he met with them. They were camped on the plain at the bottom of the mountain, and he came down on the top of the mountain in thunder, lightning, earthquake, and cloud. It was a terrifying experience. A holy God had come to meet a sinful people. And in the presence of God's holiness anything sinful is consumed. Not even the priests were allowed to step onto the mountain or else the Lord would break out against them (Ex. 19:16–24).

And yet, there on the mountain God made a covenant with his people. A covenant is a relationship-forming agreement. God promised to be their God, and they became his people. This relationship—between a holy God and sinful humanity—was possible because the covenant made provision for sin through sacrifice. Those animal sacrifices were a picture and pointer to a coming comprehensive solution. Just like at the Passover, a day was coming when God's people would be redeemed through blood. And so, as the covenant was confirmed, the blood of the sacrifice was sprinkled on the people: "Moses took the blood and threw it on the people and said, 'Behold the blood of the covenant that the LORD has made with you in accordance with all these words'" (Ex. 24:8). What happened next?

> Then Moses and Aaron, Nadab, and Abihu, and seventy of the elders of Israel went up, and they saw the God of Israel. There was under his feet as it were a pavement of sapphire stone, like the very heaven for clearness. And he did not lay his hand on the chief men of the people of Israel; they beheld God, and ate and drank. (Ex. 24:9–11)

The representatives of God's people went up the mountain—the mountain that was off limits. They saw the God of Israel—the God who might break out against them. Sinful people came before the holy God—the God who walked across the skies on a pavement of sapphire. And yet God did not raise his hand against them. Instead, what did they do? They ate and drank. This is the climax of the exodus story. This is what it has all been for. This is the epitome of divine grace: *a meal in the presence of God.*

6. The Bread of Presence: The Story of God's Presence

On the mountain, God told Moses to build a tabernacle, a sign of his presence among his people. The tabernacle had echoes of the Garden of Eden—it was decorated with fruit-bearing trees. This was God's blueprint for a new future. It was a promise of a restored creation written in architecture. The tabernacle also echoed the encounter with God at Mount Sinai. The altar of incense, for example, created a permanent cloud of smoke around the Most Holy Place, like the cloud that enveloped God on the mountain. The tabernacle recreated the story of Mount Sinai.

One of the key pieces of furniture in the tabernacle was a table overlaid with gold (Ex. 25:23–30; 37:10–16; 40:22–23). On the table was placed freshly baked bread (Lev. 24:5–9). It was there as a reminder of the meal on Mount Sinai and a promise to the renewal of that meal. What was the bread called? "The bread of the Presence" (Ex. 25:30; 35:13; 39:36). Here again is an invitation to *a meal in the presence of God.*

7. The True Happy Meal: The Story of God's Home

God gave his people the promised land. It was a land repeatedly described in terms of a menu—a land flowing with milk and honey (Ex. 3:8, 17; 13:5; 33:3; Lev. 20:24; Num. 13:27; 14:8; Deut. 6:3; 11:9: 26:9, 15; 27:3; 31:20; Josh. 5:6; Jer. 11:5; 32:22; Ezek. 20:6, 15). This is how the people are described at the high point of their life in the land, during the golden age of King Solomon: "Judah and Israel were as many as the sand by the sea. They ate and drank and were happy" (1 Kings 4:20). Here is a picture of God's salvation: people enjoying a meal in a secure home.

8. Exile and Famine: The Story of God's Judgment

The eighth meal is really no meal. God's people did not remain faithful to God. They turned to idols and practiced injustice. The result was the judgment of exile. The covenant curses kicked in, and one of those curses was famine:

> Cursed shall be the fruit of your womb and the fruit of your ground, the increase of your herds and the young of your flock. . . .

You shall carry much seed into the field and shall gather in little, for the locust shall consume it. You shall plant vineyards and dress them, but you shall neither drink of the wine nor gather the grapes, for the worm shall eat them. . . .

Because you did not serve the LORD your God with joyfulness and gladness of heart, because of the abundance of all things, therefore you shall serve your enemies whom the LORD will send against you, in hunger and thirst, in nakedness, and lacking everything. And he will put a yoke of iron on your neck until he has destroyed you. (Deut. 28:18, 38–39, 47–48)

But remember, the goal of salvation is not just food but a meal in the presence of God. In judgment, God put that hope in reverse. The prophet Joel described a locust army that would lay waste to the land (1:4–7). As a result, there would be no food to eat a meal in God's presence. The priests would wail

> because grain offering and drink offering
>> are withheld from the house of your God. (1:13)

> Is not the food cut off
>> before our eyes,
> joy and gladness
>> from the house of our God? (1:16)

The ultimate tragedy was that the people could not eat in God's presence. This is humanity's fate apart from God's grace.

9. Another Meal on a Mountain: The Story of God's Feast
But this was not the end of the story. The prophets promised a new future for God's people.

> On this mountain the LORD of hosts will make for all
>> peoples
>> a feast of rich food, a feast of well-aged wine,
>> of rich food full of marrow, of aged wine well refined.
> And he will swallow up on this mountain
>> the covering that is cast over all peoples,
>> the veil that is spread over all nations.
> He will swallow up death forever;
> and the Lord God will wipe away tears from all faces,
>> and the reproach of his people he will take away from
>>> all the earth,
>> for the LORD has spoken. (Isa. 25:6–8)

This is not just a meal but a feast. For on the menu are "rich food" and "aged wine well refined." This is not just for Israel but for "all peoples." And this is not just for a moment but for all eternity. For death itself is going to be eaten. God is going to "swallow up death forever." Our tears will be wiped away. We will eat and drink and be happy, just as Israel did during its golden age. Our *dis*-grace will be removed and replaced with grace. This is our hope: *a meal prepared by God in the presence of God.*

We cannot and do not contribute anything to this meal. The price will be paid by God himself. This one is on the house, as it were. For us there is no charge. It is covered by grace. And so in Isaiah 55:1–2 the invitations go out:

> Come, everyone who thirsts,
>> come to the waters;
> and he who has no money,
>> come, buy and eat!
> Come, buy wine and milk
>> without money and without price.

Why do you spend your money for that which is not bread,
and your labor for that which does not satisfy?
Listen diligently to me, and eat what is good,
and delight yourselves in rich food.

10. Levi's Party: The Story of God's Grace

Then we move to the home of a tax collector called Levi in first-century Judea (Luke 5:27–32). Levi is hosting a party, and the guest of honor is Jesus. The religious leaders are horrified. That's because tax collectors were collaborators with the occupying Roman army, the army that had defiled God's land. So tax collectors were not just enemies of the people; they were enemies of God. And yet, here is Jesus eating with them. Either Jesus is not the promised Messiah, or God is far more gracious than we realize. It is not even that this is a one-off incident. Robert Karris says, "In Luke's Gospel Jesus is either going to a meal, at a meal, or coming from a meal."[1] Jesus himself says the Son of Man (the term he normally used to describe himself) came "eating and drinking" (Luke 7:34). By eating with tax collectors and sinners, Jesus shows us in the most tangible way that God welcomes his enemies. This is God's grace in action.

11. The Feeding of the Five Thousand: The Story of God's Future

In Luke 9:10–17 a crowd gathers to hear Jesus teaching. Late in the afternoon the disciples urge him to call it a day so the people can disperse to find food. But instead Jesus himself feeds them using just five loaves and two fish. He provides miraculous food for the people. We are meant to think back to the provision of manna. Perhaps, too, we are to recall the high point of Israel's

---

1. Robert J. Karris, *Eating Your Way through Luke's Gospel* (Collegeville, MN: Liturgical, 2006), 14.

story when "they ate and drank and were happy" (1 Kings 4:20). Luke says, "They all ate and were satisfied" (Luke 9:17). Here, for a brief moment, is a glimpse of the fulfillment of God's promise. Jesus is the one who will provide an eternal meal in the presence of God.

12. The Last Supper and the Lord's Supper: The Whole Story in One Meal

And so we come to our final meal, the Last Supper (Luke 22:1–30). Except it is not the final meal. For the Last Supper becomes the Lord's Supper. This is the meal you and I enjoy *repeatedly*. We enter the story and become characters in the drama every time we meet around the Communion table. What Adam and Eve experienced in the garden, what the elders of Israel experienced on the mountain, what the bread of presence promised in the tabernacle is now enjoyed by the disciples in the upper room. And this is what we enjoy every time we celebrate Communion as we eat together in the presence of Christ.

It is a meal that echoes all the other meals and points to their fulfillment.

The Lord's Supper *looks back* to the Passover meal. Luke is at pains to point this out in his account of the Last Supper, mentioning the Passover in Luke 22:1, 7, 8, 11, 13, and 15. The Passover meal told the story of redemption from slavery through the blood of a lamb. The Communion meal tells the story of redemption from sin through the blood of Jesus, the Lamb of God. The Sinai covenant and its sprinkled blood find their fulfillment in the cross. This is God's complete and permanent solution for sin. All who come to Christ are cleansed by his blood and welcomed to his banquet. We are invited to eat in the presence of God. At the Last Supper, Jesus said, "This cup that is poured out for you is the new covenant in my blood" (Luke 22:20). The cup represents the new covenant, a new relationship-forming agreement through which we become God's people and he becomes our God. The Communion meal embodies the grace of God to needy sinners.

Paul would later say we "proclaim the Lord's death" every time we eat it (1 Cor. 11:26). Here in this meal we encounter the heart of our salvation. And we do not just see it or hear it. We eat it! It becomes part of us. We enact what Jesus said in John 6:51, 54–56:

> I am the living bread that came down from heaven. If anyone eats of this bread, he will live forever. And the bread that I will give for the life of the world is my flesh.
>
> . . . Whoever feeds on my flesh and drinks my blood has eternal life, and I will raise him up on the last day. For my flesh is true food, and my blood is true drink. Whoever feeds on my flesh and drinks my blood abides in me, and I in him.

This is a meal at which Jesus is the host. He tells Peter and John to "go and prepare the Passover" (Luke 22:8). But the point of their mysterious encounter with an apparently random man carrying a jar of water is to show that Jesus has made everything ready (Luke 22:7–13). It is a powerful picture of the way Jesus prepares the eternal banquet by dying in our place. He takes the judgment we deserve so we can come to eat in the presence of God. At the cross Jesus experiences exclusion from God (like Adam from the garden) and exile from God (like Israel in Babylon) so we can come close to God.

The Lord's Supper also echoes the feeding of the five thousand. That miracle involved four verbs: *taking, thanking, breaking, giving* (Luke 9:16). The same four verbs in the same order describe Jesus's consecration of the bread in Luke 22:19:

"And he took bread, and when he had given thanks, he broke it and gave it to them." Here is Jesus providing bread from heaven to satisfy his people, except that now this bread is his own body, which we feed on by faith as we consume the Communion bread.

The Lord's Supper also *points forward* to the final eternal banquet promised by Isaiah. Luke's account of the Last Supper is bookended by references to Christ's return (Luke 22:14–18, 28–30). Jesus says, "I will not eat it until it is fulfilled in the kingdom of God" (Luke 22:16; also v. 18). Just as Jesus eagerly desired to eat the *first* Lord's Supper with his friends (Luke 22:15), so now he eagerly waits to eat the *eternal* Supper with his bride. Paul would later say that in the Communion meal we proclaim the Lord's death "until he comes" (1 Cor. 11:26).

We have a preview of this future at the end of Luke's Gospel. The risen Christ meets two disciples on the road to Emmaus and shows them from the Scriptures that it was necessary for the Christ to suffer before entering his glory (Luke 24:25–27). At the end of the journey they sit down to a meal together. "When he was at table with them, he took the bread and blessed and broke it and gave it to them. And their eyes were opened, and they recognized him" (Luke 24:30–31). Again, it is the same sequence of four verbs as Luke used to describe the feeding of the five thousand and the Last Supper: *took, blessed, broke, gave* (cf. Luke 9:16; 22:19). The meal in Emmaus is not the great messianic banquet, but it is, along with the Lord's Supper, a glimpse of the future. A few verses later Luke tells us that the disciples "gave him a piece of broiled fish, and he took it and ate before them" (Luke 24:42–43). The words "before them" are significant. The physicality of the body of the risen Christ becomes clear.

It is a picture of our future, for Christ has risen as the first-fruits of all his people. Our future is a meal in resurrected physical bodies in the presence of Christ.

So baptism and Communion point to the resurrection of our bodies and the renewal of creation. Baptism involves getting wet with water, and Communion involves ingesting bread and wine because we are people with bodies. Our bodies are not secondary or incidental to our identity. And our bodies are part of our future. We believe in the bodily resurrection of Jesus, who rose as the firstborn of the new creation. So, believe in the redemption of our bodies. The physicality of Communion is a reminder of the physicality of salvation.

"Blessed are those," says the angel of Revelation 19:9, "who are invited to the marriage supper of the Lamb!" Every time we take Communion together, we anticipate this messianic banquet. Indeed, we do not just remember the banquet when we take Communion. We get a little foretaste—a "before taste"—of heaven.

It is appropriate that sometimes our Communion meals, or components of them, are solemn moments in which we lament our sin and remember the price Christ paid for our salvation. But there should also be exuberant moments in which we anticipate the joy and plenty of the eternal banquet. Communion does not have to involve a tiny morsel of bread and the smallest cup in town. The early church celebrated Communion in the context of a love feast.

At the same time, the Supper reminds us that this messianic banquet has not yet come, and at the moment Jesus is physically absent. "For I tell you," says Jesus, "that from now on I will not drink of the fruit of the vine until the kingdom of God comes" (Luke 22:18). The Supper points us to the banquet, but it also reminds us that we are not there yet. In this way, it acts as a check on any triumphalism. It reminds us that we still live in an as-yet-unredeemed world, scarred by sin and in desperate need of the gospel. Even as it satisfies our spiritual hunger, it instills in us a longing for the day when we will commune with our Savior face-to-face.

Every Communion Meal Is a Participation in God's Grace

In the house of Levi, Jesus ate with God's enemies. And at every Communion, Jesus welcomes us to the table. He invites his enemies to become his friends. He is the host and we are his guests. "Isn't it amazing," says Ligon Duncan, "that we're invited to slide our knees up under the table of God?"[2] Every Communion is an embodiment of God's grace. We hear God's grace in the words that are spoken. But we also see it, hear it, touch it, and taste it in the bread and wine. *God in his kindness, knowing how frail we are, knowing how battered by life we can be, also demonstrates his grace in water, bread, and wine.*

We are embodied beings. We are not minds that just happen to have bodies. That is the ancient heresy of dualism. Nor are our bodies temporary. Christians believe in the resurrection of the body to eternal life. So our bodies are an intrinsic part of who we are. And therefore God communicates not just to minds but to embodied souls. The church father Chrysostom puts it like this: "If we were incorporeal [without bodies], he would give us these very things naked and incorporeal. Now, because we have souls engrafted in bodies, he imparts spiritual things under visible ones."[3] The sacraments are, as it were, God's "body

---

2. Ligon Duncan, in *The New City Catechism Devotional: God's Truth for Our Hearts and Minds*, ed. Collin Hansen (Wheaton, IL: Crossway, 2017), 201.

3. Chrysostom, cited in John Calvin, *Institutes of the Christian Religion*, ed. John T. McNeill, trans. Ford Lewis Battles, Library of Christian Classics 20–21 (Philadelphia: Westminster, 1960), 4.14.3.

language." We pick up signals from people's posture and facial expressions that often reinforce their words. The sacraments are given to confirm the words we hear in the gospel.

The Communion meal involves us in and embraces us in God's grace. We are not mere observers. We do something. We eat something. We become participants in the story. Again and again John Calvin speaks of the Supper as a banquet in which we feed on Christ. "Our souls are fed by the flesh and blood of Christ," he says, "in the same way that bread and wine keep and sustain physical life."[4] The French Confession of Faith of 1559 says, "The body and the blood of Jesus Christ give food and drink to the soul, no less than bread and wine nourish the body" (§37). We are often quick to talk about being fed by the word of God, or we pray that we might be fed by the word as it is preached. In the same way, we can be fed by Communion. As physical food, bread and wine satisfy our bodies with carbohydrates, sugars, and nutrients; as spiritual food, they satisfy our souls with Christ. In the liturgy Calvin wrote for the celebration of Communion in Geneva, he included these words of invitation:

> Let us understand, therefore, that this Sacrament is a medicine for poor, spiritually sick people. . . . And since we see only bread and wine, yet we do not doubt that he accomplishes spiritually in our souls all that he demonstrates to us outwardly through these visible signs, namely, that he is the heavenly bread that feeds and nourishes us for eternal life. So let us be grateful for the infinite goodness of our Saviour, who spreads out all his riches and goods on this table to distribute them to us.[5]

---

4. Calvin, *Institutes*, 4.17.10.

5. John Calvin, "Form of Ecclesiastical Prayers (1545, 1542, 1566)," in *Reformation Worship: Liturgies from the Past for the Present*, ed. Jonathan Gibson and Mark Earngey (Greensboro, NC: New Growth, 2018), 327.

The Westminster Confession has this to say: "Worthy receivers, outwardly partaking of the visible elements, in this sacrament, do then also, inwardly by faith, really and indeed, yet not carnally and corporally but spiritually, receive, and feed upon, Christ crucified, and all benefits of his death" (29.7). The 1689 Baptist Confession of Faith uses these exact same words, except that it replaces the word "sacrament" with "ordinance" (30.7). The Westminster Confession says much the same thing about baptism:

> The efficacy of Baptism is not tied to that moment of time wherein it is administered; yet, notwithstanding, by the right use of this ordinance, the grace promised is not only offered, but really exhibited, and conferred, by the Holy Ghost, to such (whether of age or infants) as that grace belongs unto, according to the counsel of God's own will, in His appointed time. (28.6)

Notice how strong this language is: grace is "conferred" through baptism. That does not mean someone is automatically saved simply by being baptized—that is why the confession says, "The efficacy of Baptism is not tied to that moment of time wherein it is administered." Nevertheless, when someone responds with faith to the promises expressed in baptism, that is an act of regenerating grace from which flows justifying grace. Grace is thereby conferred through baptism (alongside the preaching of God's word) if and when a person responds with faith.

Every meal—not just Communion, but including Communion—is a reminder that we are dependent on God as *creatures*. We are not self-sustaining. Much of our food is grown, processed, distributed, and possibly cooked by other people. We are part of a complex web of relationships upon which we rely day by day. And behind them all is our loving Creator, who generously provides for the needs of his creation. This is why Jesus taught us to pray, "Give us this day our daily bread" (Matt. 6:11).

But the Communion meal is special. For Communion is *also* a recognition that we are dependent on God not just as creatures but also as *sinners*. We live through the death of his Son. Each mouthful is a reminder that we cannot save ourselves. Just as we rely on daily bread for physical life, so we rely on Jesus for spiritual life. For he is the bread of life. We come to Communion as sinners in desperate need of reassurance, and we hear the words, "This is my blood of the covenant, which is poured out for many for the forgiveness of sins" (Matt. 26:28).

The Belgic Confession of 1516 says that people who have been born again have a twofold life: a bodily life and a spiritual life. Like everyone else, their physical life is nourished by physical food. But God also gives his children spiritual food in Christ, the bread of life, to nourish their spiritual life. And we receive this food through the bread and wine of Communion.

> Christ, that he might represent unto us this spiritual and heavenly bread, has instituted an earthly and visible bread, as a sacrament of his body, and wine as a sacrament of his blood, to testify by them unto us, that, as certainly as we receive and hold this sacrament in our hands, and eat and drink the same with our mouths, by which our life is afterwards nourished, we also do as certainly receive by faith (which is the hand and mouth of our soul) the true body and blood of Christ our only Saviour in our souls, for the support of our spiritual life.... This feast is a spiritual

table, at which Christ communicates himself with all his benefits to us. (§35)

Frances Turretin adds a key difference between physical and spiritual food: "Corporal food is converted into our substance, while spiritual food, because more powerful and perfect, changes us in some way into his substance, so that we become confirmed to Christ and live the life of Christ and are made partakers of the divine nature (2 Pet. 1:4)."[6]

Means of Grace

Catholicism, says Calvin, wrongly *confuses* the signs (the water, bread, and wine) with the reality to which they point (Christ and his benefits). According to Catholicism the bread is Christ; the sign is the thing it signifies. But some Protestants, says Calvin, go too far in the opposite direction. They wrongly *separate* the signs from the reality. Calvin himself advocated a middle position that kept signs and reality united without confusing them. The signs actually *convey* the reality to which they point when received by faith. Baptism and Communion are a genuine means of grace or communion. "Bare forms are not exhibited to us in the sacraments, but the reality is truly figured at the same time. For God is not so deceitful as to nourish us in empty appearances. . . . We have no right to separate the reality and the figure which God has joined together."[7] In other words, the signs *convey* the reality they signify without *becoming* the reality they signify.

The 1559 French (or Gallic) Confession of Faith says, "We hold that [the sacraments'] substance and truth is in Jesus

---

6. Francis Turretin, *Institutes of Elenctic Theology*, trans. George Musgrave Giger, ed. James T. Dennison Jr., vol. 3 (Phillipsburg, NJ: P&R, 1997), 432.

7. John Calvin, *Commentary on 1 Corinthians*, ed. Thomas F. Torrance and David W. Torrance, trans. John W. Fraser (Grand Rapids, MI: Eerdmans, 1980), 203.

Christ, and that of themselves they are only smoke and shadow." Nevertheless, "they are outward signs through which God operates by his Spirit, so that he may not signify any thing to us in vain" (§34). In other words, through the Spirit the signs (the water, bread, and wine) convey the reality (Christ) to us when we receive them by faith. "God gives us really and in fact that which he there sets forth to us" (§37). "By the secret and incomprehensible power of his Spirit he feeds and strengthens us with the substance of his body and of his blood" (§36).

As I pass the bread to you, I can rightly say, "This is the body of Christ, given for you." This does not mean the sign has turned into the thing it signifies. The bread has not become Christ's physical body. If it did, it would stop being a sign or sacrament, for it would be the reality itself. Nevertheless, the signs are "mystical tokens of holy things" because the sign and the signified are "sacramentally joined together" by God so that the sign conveys what it signifies (the presence of Christ) (Second Helvetic Confession, 19.9). Likewise the Westminster Confession says, "Truly, yet sacramentally only, they are sometimes called by the name of the things they represent" (29.5). In other words, the bread and wine are called the body and blood of Christ, even though they remain only bread and wine, because they genuinely convey the presence of Christ. The Westminster Confession concludes, "There is, in every sacrament, a spiritual relation, or sacramental union, between the sign and the thing signified: whence it comes to pass, that the names and effects of the one are attributed to the other" (27.2; see also 29.5).

If you find the technicalities of this discussion somewhat confusing, here is what it boils down to. When we receive the water, bread, and wine by faith, we receive the grace of God. God has committed himself to use the water, bread, and wine—along with his word—to bless his people. This is how our faith is strengthened. This is how we receive assurance of salvation. This is how we have communion with Christ. As Calvin keeps reminding us, in the Lord's Supper we truly feed on Christ by faith, and in this way he nourishes our souls. In theory, God could zap us directly with his power. But he has committed himself to use word, water, bread, and wine. And so, ordinarily he uses these ordinary means.

This means if you want to receive God's blessing, you do not need to go looking for some dramatic new experience. The place to be is your local church, where the word is proclaimed and the sacraments are administered. You simply need to read your Bible, listen to expository preaching week by week, and participate in the Lord's Supper. This is where God's grace to us in Christ is found.

Part of our problem is that we too often view preaching as primarily conveying information about Christ rather than conveying the grace of Christ. If that is the case, it is no surprise that we then have a problem with the sacraments, since it is not obvious how they convey information—other than as a prompt for remembering what has already been said. The Reformers, in contrast, had a high view of preaching, in which God was present in and through his word. Here's how Martin Luther put it: "I preach the gospel of Christ, and with my bodily voice I bring Christ into your heart, so that you may hear from him within yourself." As a result, we have "the true Christ." "How that comes about you cannot know, but your heart truly feels his presence, and through the experience of faith you know for a certainty that he is there. . . . This we must ever confess, and it is a daily miracle."[8] Given this view of preaching, it was not hard

---

8. Martin Luther, *The Sacrament of the Body and Blood—Against the Fanatics*, in *Martin Luther's Basic Theological Writings*, 3rd ed., ed. Timothy F. Lull (Minneapolis: Fortress, 2012), 227.

for the Reformers to recognize that something similar happens in Communion. Just as we encounter Christ and his promise in his word, so we also encounter him in Communion. Luther goes on, "Why then should it not be reasonable that he also distributes himself in the bread?"[9]

Sometimes people ask, "Do you need to be baptized to be saved?" It is one of those questions like "Have you stopped beating your wife?" that cannot be answered yes or no. That's because it is the wrong question. It views baptism simply as a requirement and asks whether this requirement is essential to salvation. But baptism is, above all, a gift we receive from God. Baptism and Communion are key means that God uses to convey grace to his people to nurture our faith in his promises and to strengthen our sense of his love. Most Christians do not ask, "Do you need to listen to preaching each week to be saved?" We love to hear God's word because it reassures and sustains us. It is the same with the sacraments. So the real question is not, "Do you need to be baptized to be saved?" but, "Do you want an amazing gift?"

Every Meal Can Be a Witness to God's Grace

So the Lord's Supper embodies and conveys God's grace to us. But it can also, therefore, become a model for our everyday suppers. What we learn and practice around the Communion table is meant to spill out into the rest of our lives. The grace we receive at Communion is meant to shape the way we relate to other people.

One of the main ways we can do that is through meals. The saying of grace at every family meal is energized by the focus on grace at the Communion meal. Every meal becomes

---

9. Luther, *The Sacrament of the Body and Blood*, 227.

an occasion for *gratitude*. But Communion also helps our meals become occasions for *giving*. Meals are a powerful expression of welcome and friendship in every culture. So eating with people creates community and proclaims grace. This was how Jesus conducted his ministry on earth. Meals are a wonderful way of doing ministry.

Here is the beauty of it: you are already doing it. You are already eating two or three meals a day. Ministry through meals does not require special skills or additional time. No matter who you are or how busy you are, you can eat with people. It does not have to be fancy hospitality. It is about inviting people into your home to share your family meals. As you do that, relationships will form, stories will be told, conversation will develop, testimonies will be shared, grace will be demonstrated.

The story of salvation is the story of meals. It is a narrative embodied in the Communion meal. And we can continue the story through *our* meals. Every meal can embody something of God's grace and enact something of God's mission. If you combine sharing meals with a passion for Jesus, then you will be doing mission and building community. In our graceless culture of competition, insecurity, and grudges, our meals offer a moment of grace and a pointer to God's coming world.

Come, You Sinners, Poor and Needy

Perhaps we have grown too used to Communion, and so we miss the wonder of what is happening. Think of those Israel elders stepping onto Mount Sinai. What had they experienced of God? "Now when all the people saw the thunder and the flashes of lightning and the sound of the trumpet and the mountain smoking, the people were afraid and trembled, and they stood far off and said to Moses, 'You speak to us, and we will listen; but do not let God speak to us, lest we die'" (Ex. 20:18–19). Yet the elders are going up the mountain to face *that* God. And because they are sprinkled with blood, God does not raise his hand. Instead, they eat and drink in his presence. That is what happens every time we take Communion: covered by the blood of Christ, we eat in the presence of God. The grace of God is embodied in a meal.

Or think of John Paton, a missionary in the nineteenth century to cannibals in the New Hebrides. At numerous times they tried to kill him. Yet he remained, and after years of patient, faithful witness, many came to Christ. Here's how Paton describes their first Communion:

> For years we had toiled and prayed and taught for this. At the moment when I put the bread and wine into those dark hands, once stained with the blood of cannibalism but now stretched out to receive and partake the emblems and seals of the Redeemer's love, I had a foretaste of the joy of glory that well-nigh broke my heart to pieces. I shall never taste a deeper bliss till I gaze on the glorified face of Jesus himself.[10]

We are no different from the elders of Israel stepping onto the mountain or the tax collectors in Levi's house or the former cannibals of the New Hebrides. We are sinners who deserve divine judgment. Yet all of us find a welcome when we come to the table in faith and repentance.

Joseph Hart (1712–1768) was converted in 1757 through the preaching of George Whitefield, one of the leaders of the

---

10. James Paton, ed., *John G. Paton—Missionary to the New Hebrides: An Autobiography* (London: Hodder and Stoughton, 1891), 376, quoted in Philip Graham Ryken, *Exodus: Saved for God's Glory* (Wheaton, IL: Crossway, 2005), 915.

Great Awakening. Here's how he expresses Christ's invitation to sinners:

> Come, ye sinners, poor and needy,
> weak and wounded, sick and sore;
> Jesus ready stands to save you,
> full of pity, love and power:
> he is able, he is able,
> he is willing; doubt no more.
>
> Now, ye needy, come and welcome;
> God's free bounty glorify;
> true belief and true repentance,
> every grace that brings you nigh.
> Without money, without money,
> come to Jesus Christ and buy....
>
> Come, ye weary, heavy-laden,
> lost and ruined by the Fall.
> If you wait until you're better,
> you will never come at all.
> Not the righteous, not the righteous—
> sinners Jesus came to call.
>
> View him prostrate in the garden;
> on the ground your Maker lies!
> On the awful tree behold him,
> hear him cry before he dies:
> It is finished! It is finished!
> Sinner, will not this suffice?
>
> Lo, the incarnate God, ascended,
> pleads the merit of his blood.
> Venture on him, venture wholly,
> let not other trust intrude.

None but Jesus, none but Jesus
can do helpless sinners good.[11]

Here is how Jesus himself expressed that invitation to the lukewarm church of Laodicea: "Behold, I stand at the door and knock. If anyone hears my voice and opens the door, I will come in to him and eat with him, and he with me" (Rev. 3:20).

---

11. Joseph Hart, "Come, Ye Sinners, Poor and Needy" (1759), in *Grace Hymns*, 2nd ed. (London: Grace Publications Trust, 1978), no. 389.

3

ENACTED PRESENCE

One of the things we often say is that we should find satisfaction in Christ. "Christ is enough," we tell one another.

But imagine a single woman walking home from a party. Ahead is an empty house and an empty bed. What she leaves behind, perhaps, is the potential to be embraced by a man (a man to whom she is not married), to feel his touch, to feel the taste of his kiss on her lips. "Christ is enough" may be true. But what does Christ *feel* like? How can he compete with the touch of another human being? How is satisfaction in Christ to be tangible? Or is satisfaction in Christ a mental exercise, maybe even an act of make believe? As a pastoral colleague once asked me after describing just such a scenario, "In that moment what does Christ *taste* like?"

One of the words we use to describe the Lord's Supper is Communion. It comes from 1 Corinthians 10:16, which describes the cup as "a participation in the blood of Christ" and the bread as "a participation in the body of Christ." The word "participation" translates the Greek word *koinōnia*, which means "communion" or "fellowship." It conveys the idea that the Supper is an act of communion or participation with Christ—and also with one another. It is a relational act.

Meals are often like that. Think what an invitation to dinner means. It is more than an invitation to food; it is an invitation to friendship. The Lord's Supper is an invitation to friendship with Christ. It is an invitation to experience Christ's presence.

But what does that mean? How is Christ present at the Lord's Supper? This has been a controversial question over the years.

Catholicism: The Bread and Wine Become the Body and Blood of Christ

In the parish church in the village of Eyam near where I used to live, a long hole runs through the wall where the nave, the area where people sit, meets the chancel, the area with the Communion table. This hole is called a "squint." At present it enables those in the south aisle to see through the wall into the chancel. But when it was originally built, there was no south aisle, and instead it led outside. Outcasts within the community might not be willing or welcome to join the congregation inside the building. But seven hundred years ago, at the crucial moment they could look through the squint to see the minister holding up the bread. This was the moment you wanted to see, because in this moment Christ became *physically* present in the bread and wine. Christ himself had appeared in your little country parish. That is why the squint was built.

The traditional Catholic view is that the outward appearance of the bread remains unchanged, but its inner essence becomes the real, physical body of Christ. It may still look and taste like bread, but its inner essence is now that of Christ's body. This belief is known as "transubstantiation," because the substance (the inner essence) of the bread is said to transform.

This remains official Catholic teaching to this day. The contemporary Catechism of the Catholic Church says:

> By the consecration the transubstantiation of the bread and wine into the Body and Blood of Christ is brought about. Under the consecrated species of bread and wine Christ himself, living and glorious, is present in a true, real, and substantial manner: his Body and his Blood, with his soul and his divinity. (§1413)

So complete is the transformation supposed to be that the bread and wine are said to cease to exist: they have been entirely replaced by the body and blood of Christ.

Transubstantiation goes far beyond anything taught in the Bible and instead relies heavily on categories from the Greek philosophy of Aristotle. But it is important to recognize that it is an earnest attempt to work out how Christ is present at the Lord's Supper. Transubstantiation is also sometimes known as belief in "real presence," though this is somewhat misleading, since the Reformed position also believes Christ is really present at the Supper. The difference is that Catholicism believes Christ is *physically* present in the bread, whereas Reformed theology believes, as we shall see, that he is *spiritually* present through the Holy Spirit.

More problematic are two related Catholic ideas. First, the Catholic Church teaches that the sacraments convey God's grace *ex opere operato*—"by the action of the act," irrespective of whether there is faith. The water, bread, and wine are viewed as if they are medicine with the power to transform a person, whether or not that person understands what is happening or is trusting in Christ. This was developed to justify baptismal regeneration, the idea that babies become Christians simply through the act of being baptized (hence the term "Christening," which means "Christian making"). This is linked to a Catholic view of grace. Grace is not seen as a relational quality—God's undeserved kindness toward his people. Instead, it is seen as a "thing" that can be transmitted through the sacraments—a kind of power or boost that God gives to help us become righteous people. Instead of our being made right with God through faith in the finished work of Christ, Catholic theology teaches that righteousness is a power infused into us through baptism and topped up through Communion, which boosts our attempt to live a life that might perhaps find acceptance before God.

Second, the Catholic Church teaches that Christ is offered afresh or "re-presented" at Communion. The word "host," used in Catholic theology to describe the Communion bread, comes from a Latin word (*hostia*), which means "sacrificial victim." Quoting the Council of Trent (the Catholic Church's sixteenth-century response to the Reformation), the Catechism of the Catholic Church says:

> The Eucharist is also a sacrifice.... In the Eucharist Christ gives us the very body which he gave up for us on the cross, the very blood which he "poured out for many for the forgiveness of sins." (§1365)

> "The victim is one and the same: the same now offers through the ministry of priests, who then offered himself on the cross; only the manner of the offering is different." "... in this divine sacrifice which is celebrated in the Mass, the same Christ who offered himself once in a bloody manner on the altar of the cross is contained and is offered in an unbloody manner." (§1367)

The problem with this is that in the popular imagination it risks undermining the sufficiency of the cross. On the cross Christ cried, "It is finished" (John 19:30). The writer of Hebrews expresses the completed work of Christ by comparing it to the repeated offerings of the Old Testament priests:

> And every priest stands daily at his service, offering repeatedly the same sacrifices, which can never take away sins. But when Christ had offered for all time a single sacrifice for sins, he sat down at the right hand of God, waiting from that time until his enemies should be made a footstool for his feet. For by a single offering he has perfected for all time those who are being sanctified. (10:11–14)

The significance of this is clear. Christ's sacrifice is complete. It need not and cannot be repeated by a priest. Despite this evidence of the complete and sufficient work of the cross, the Catholic understanding of the Lord's Supper implies that Christ's atoning work must be continually performed by a priest. Martin Luther described this teaching as "the greatest blasphemy and abomination ever known on the earth." "It is quite certain," he said, "that Christ cannot be sacrificed over and above the one single time he sacrificed himself."[1]

Luther: Christ Is Physically Present in the Communion Bread and Wine

Nevertheless, like Catholicism, Luther also believed Christ is physically present in Communion, albeit invisibly. In Communion, he said, Christ "is just as near to us bodily as he was" to those who saw, heard, and touched him when he lived on earth.[2] "There is only one body of Christ, which both mouth and heart

---

1. Martin Luther, "That These Words of Christ, 'This Is My Body,' etc., Still Stand Firm against the Fanatics" (1527), ed. Amy Nelson Burnett, in *The Annotated Luther*, vol. 3, *Church and Sacraments*, ed. Paul W. Robinson (Minneapolis: Fortress, 2016), 269.

2. Luther, "That These Words of Christ," 235.

eat, each in its own mode."[3] This view of Christ's presence in Communion is known as "consubstantiation." The prefix *con-* means "with." In his Large Catechism, Luther says, "The true body and blood of the Lord Christ" is "in and under the bread and wine."[4] Lutheranism would go on to speak of the body of Christ being present "under the bread, with the bread, in the bread."[5] The bread and wine do not change, but the substance of Christ's physical body is present with or alongside the bread and wine. Luther refused to budge from a literal interpretation of "This is my body" (Luke 22:19).

Luther's primary emphasis was on the power of the word: "It is not his body and blood except by his Word."[6] This did not mean the word of the priest somehow magically invoked Christ. It is the word or promise *of God* (repeated by the minister) through which Christ is bodily present. Unlike Catholicism, Luther believed faith is vital—word and sacrament must go together. Indeed, he said that if the bread and wine are received without faith, then they are "poisonous and deadly."[7]

Luther's explanation for how consubstantiation happened went like this. At the incarnation the divine Son of God took on a human body; Christ was one person with a divine nature and a human nature. After his ascension the qualities of his divine nature were "communicated" to his human nature so that what is true of his divine nature can now also be true of his human nature. This means his omniscience (his presence everywhere) is added to his humanity. As a result, in a myste-

---

3. Luther, "That These Words of Christ," 234.

4. Martin Luther, "The Large Catechism," in *The Book of Concord* (1580), ed. Robert Kolb and Timothy J. Wengert (Minneapolis: Fortress, 2000), pt. 5, §8 (467).

5. "The Solid Declaration of the Formula of Concord," in *The Book of Concord*, 599.

6. Martin Luther, *WA* 30.1:23, 34–35, quoted in Thomas J. Davis, *This Is My Body: The Presence of Christ in Reformation Thought* (Grand Rapids, MI: Baker, 2008), 47.

7. Luther, "That These Words of Christ," 228; see also John Calvin, *Institutes of the Christian Religion*, ed. John T. McNeill, trans. Ford Lewis Battles, Library of Christian Classics 20–21 (Philadelphia: Westminster, 1960), 4.17.10.

rious way Christ's body is physically present everywhere and especially in Communion (an idea known as the "ubiquity" of Christ's humanity).

Zwingli: The Bread and Wine Remind Us of Christ's Death

The Swiss Reformer Huldrych Zwingli agreed with much of Luther's critique of Catholic theology. But he and Luther radically disagreed on the nature of Communion. Zwingli believed Luther's understanding confused Christ's divine and human natures. Christ's human body cannot be everywhere and still be truly human.

While Luther emphasized the words "This is my body," Zwingli emphasized the words "Do this in remembrance of me" (Luke 22:19). The bread is not the literal body of Christ, but a *reminder* of his body given for us. The words "This is my body" should not be taken literally. They do not mean Jesus is literally present in the bread any more than the words "I am the true vine" (John 15:1) mean Jesus is literally a plant. Zwingli described the Supper as a memorial.[8] It is an act we perform to remember what Christ has done for us. "The bread is only a figure of his body to remind us in the Supper that the body was crucified for us."[9]

The two sides came together at the Colloquy of Marburg in 1529. On fourteen major points Luther and Zwingli agreed. But on the fifteenth and final point, the Lord's Supper, they could not agree. On the final day Zwingli demanded a Scripture passage to prove Luther's contention that Christ was physically present in the bread. At this point Luther dramatically whipped

---

8. Huldrych Zwingli, "On the Lord's Supper" (1526), in *Zwingli and Bullinger*, ed. G. W. Bromiley, Library of Christian Classics 24 (Philadelphia: Westminster, 1953), 229.

9. Zwingli, "On the Lord's Supper," 225.

aside the table cloth to reveal words he had previously marked on the surface: *Hoc est corpus meum,* the Latin for "This is my body." "Here is our Scripture passage," Luther cried. "You have not yet taken it from us, as you set out to do; we need no other."[10] The meeting broke up with Zwingli in tears.

Zwingli saw the sacraments as a pledge of our commitment to Christ. He compared them to the white cross worn by soldiers of the Swiss Confederate army, a symbol that indicated their allegiance to the cause. The sacraments are an act we perform rather than something offered to us by Christ. In Zwingli's view, the active agents in Communion are we believers (we are the ones doing the remembering) rather than Christ (whose actions lie in the past). We remember Christ's suffering to renew our motivation to obey him. This approach to the sacraments has therefore tended to be popular in Arminian churches, which emphasize human decision-making in salvation.

There is some evidence that at the end of his life Zwingli had moved away from this position or indeed may have always seen Communion as more than a mere memorial.[11] Nevertheless, Zwingli's emphasis on remembrance has become widespread in many contemporary evangelical churches.

Calvin: Christ Is Spiritually Present at Communion through the Holy Spirit

Half a generation later, John Calvin developed an approach that mediated between Luther and Zwingli. He rejected Luther's belief that Christ's physical body was present in Communion.

---

10. Quoted in Timothy George, *Theology of the Reformers* (Leicester: Apollos, 1988), 151.

11. See, for example, Bruce A. Ware, "The Meaning of the Lord's Supper in the Theology of Ulrich Zwingli (1484–1531)," in *The Lord's Supper: Remembering and Proclaiming Christ until He Comes,* ed. Thomas R. Schreiner and Matthew R. Crawford (Nashville: B&H Academic, 2010), 229–47.

This, argued Calvin, dissolves Christ's humanity into his divinity. Instead, Calvin said that on earth Christ is now physically absent (as he said he would be in passages like John 16:28) because his human body has ascended into heaven. Indeed, if the bread is his literal flesh and the blood is his literal blood, then, says Calvin, we are left with the "absurd" idea that Christ's body and blood are in two different places, the one on the plate and the other in the cup.[12]

But Calvin also rejected Zwingli's understanding of Communion as simply a memorial act. Christ really is present in Communion. He is present to convey both his benefits (to strengthen the faith of believers) and himself (in an act of genuine communion). "The language is figurative," summarizes B. A. Gerrish; "the communication is real."[13]

But if Christ is not physically present, how is he present? Calvin answered by saying Christ is present *spiritually*—that is, through the Holy Spirit.

> The sharing in the Lord's body, which, I maintain, is offered to us in the Supper, demands neither a local presence, nor the descent of Christ, nor an infinite extension of His body, nor anything of that sort; for, in view of the fact that the Supper is a heavenly act, there is nothing absurd about saying that Christ remains in heaven and is yet received by us. For the way in which He imparts Himself to us is by the secret power of the Holy Spirit, a power which is able not only to bring together, but also to join together, things which are separated by distance, and by a great distance at that.[14]

---

12. Calvin, *Institutes*, 4.17.18; see also 4.17.23.

13. B. A. Gerrish, *Grace and Gratitude: The Eucharistic Theology of John Calvin* (Eugene, OR: Wipf and Stock, 1993), 6.

14. John Calvin, *The First Epistle of Paul the Apostle to the Corinthians*, ed. David W. Torrance and Thomas F. Torrance, trans. John W. Fraser (Edinburgh: Saint Andrews Press, 1960), 247.

The Spirit mediates the presence of Christ by bridging the distance between the ascended Christ in heaven and his people on earth. It is not that Christ's body exists somewhere among the stars. "Separation from Christ is not a function of distance; rather, distance is a metaphor for separation," says Thomas Davis. "The notion of distance was Calvin's way of speaking about the radical divide that separates the heavenly from the earthly, the divine from the human."[15] At Communion, then, the Spirit connects the heavenly and earthly realms, which are ordinarily separated spheres of existence.

As a result, Christ really is present with us in the Supper, and he really does feed our hearts by his presence. Christ "feeds his people with his own body, the communion of which he bestows upon them by the power of his Spirit."[16] If this "seems unbelievable," says Calvin, then "let us remember how far the secret power of the Holy Spirit towers above our senses, and how foolish it is to wish to measure his immeasurableness by our measure."[17] Thomas Cranmer also took this approach. Physically Christ sits beside the Father, he said, but spiritually he sits among his people:

> My doctrine is, that the very body of Christ, which was born of the virgin Mary, and suffered for our sins, giving us life by his death, the same Jesus, as concerning his bodily presence, is taken from us, and sits at the right hand of his Father. And yet is he by faith spiritually present with us, and is our spiritual food and nourishment, and sits in the midst of all who gather together in his name.[18]

---

15. Davis, *This Is My Body*, 136–37.
16. Calvin, *Institutes*, 4.17.18.
17. Calvin, *Institutes*, 4.17.10.
18. Thomas Cranmer, "Answer to Gardiner," in *The Works of Thomas Cranmer*, vol. 1, *On the Sacrament of the Lord's Supper*, ed. John Edmund Cox (Cambridge: Parker Society, 1844), 184, modernized.

The Anabaptist Menno Simons emphasizes the role of the Supper as a "memorial."[19] But he, too, says that whenever the Supper is celebrated, "Jesus Christ is present with His grace, Spirit, and promise, and with the merits of His sufferings, misery, flesh, blood, cross, and death." Simons does add an important Anabaptist qualification: the Supper must be celebrated with "faith, love, attentiveness, peace, unity of heart and mind."[20]

This understanding of Christ's spiritual presence is reflected in the confessions of Reformed churches. The Second Helvetic Confession of 1566, for example, says:

> The body of Christ is in the heavens, at the right hand of the Father; and therefore our hearts are to be lifted up on high, and not to be fixed on the bread, neither is the Lord to be worshipped in the bread. Yet the Lord is not absent from his Church when she celebrates the Supper. The sun, being absent from us in the heavens, is yet, notwithstanding, present among us effectually: how much more Christ, the Sun of Righteousness, though in body he be absent from us in the heavens, yet is present among us, not corporeally [bodily], but spiritually. (21.10)

It was also the position of the Reformed Baptist Charles H. Spurgeon, who wrote, "We firmly believe in the real presence of Christ which is spiritual, and yet certain."[21]

Present in the Act of Communion

We must not look at what happens to the bread and wine in isolation. If we do, the choice becomes either believing Christ is

---

19. Menno Simons, *The Complete Writings of Menno Simons*, ed. John C. Wenger (Scottdale, PA: Herald, 1956), 143.

20. Simons, *The Complete Writings*, 148.

21. Charles H. Spurgeon, *Till He Come* (London: Passmore and Alabaster, 1894), 17.

present in the bread or believing he is absent. But bread and wine are not to be seen in isolation from the community of Communion.

This idea is central to Paul's argument in 1 Corinthians 8–10. At first it might seem this has little to do with Communion. But stay with me and you will see that this is where it leads us.

Paul opens this section with the words "Now concerning food offered to idols" (8:1). Here is the issue. Often the meat in the markets of Corinth had previously been offered to idols in pagan ceremonies. It was offered to the gods on a Sunday and offered to customers in the butcher's shop on a Monday. Imagine you are inviting a few friends from church over for a meal. You want to give them roast lamb, roast potatoes, a vegetable, gravy, and, of course, mint sauce. So you go to the market to buy a shoulder of lamb. But as you stand in the butcher's shop, you have a crisis of conscience. What if yesterday this meat was offered to an idol? Does that matter? Has the meat transformed into something dangerous? Will eating it corrupt you or compromise you? Will it imply you've participated in pagan worship? What do you do?

The church was divided. Some said it was okay; others disagreed. It is likely the Christians in Corinth wrote to Paul asking for his advice. Here is the heart of Paul's response:

> Therefore, as to the eating of food offered to idols, we know that "an idol has no real existence," and that "there is no God but one." For although there may be so-called gods in heaven or on earth—as indeed there are many "gods" and many "lords"—yet for us there is one God, the Father, from whom are all things and for whom we exist, and one Lord, Jesus Christ, through whom are all things and through whom we exist. (8:4–6)

Paul says an idol is nothing because there is only one God. Clearly there is a sense in which there are many "gods," since we can readily name a few: Jupiter, Mars, Zeus, Allah, Krishna, Buddha. But they're not *real* gods. The only real God is God the Father and Jesus Christ.

The implication is clear. If gods are not real, then they cannot change lumps of meat. Meat offered in pagan ceremonies is unaffected. It does not change into something else. It's just meat. So eating meat bought in the market is fine. "Food will not commend us to God. We are no worse off if we do not eat, and no better off if we do" (8:8).

Now, Paul is careful to qualify this. We must not pressure a brother or sister to act against his or her conscience. That would not be loving. Knowledge without love is not really knowledge (8:1–3). You may know that it's okay to eat meat that has been offered to idols. But real knowledge is to know God or, rather, to be known by God (8:3). Real knowledge is relational. So if you are really "in the know," then you will love your brothers and sisters. You will not parade your knowledge, nor will you encourage others to sin against their consciences. So Paul says that eating meat is fine *unless* doing so causes another Christian to sin against his or her conscience (8:9–13). "But take care that this right of yours does not somehow become a stumbling block to the weak," says Paul in verse 9. We should not always insist on our rights, he says, using his own attitude toward his rights as an apostle as a case study in chapter 9. Paul gave up his rights to make it easier for people to hear the gospel. "For though I am free from all, I have made myself a servant to all, that I might win more of them" (9:19).

Despite these qualifications, the principle is clear: eating meat offered to idols is fine because the meat does not change into something evil.

But then in chapter 10, Paul returns to the issue of food and drink, and it looks like he has changed his tune. This time he has a warning. He says the people of Israel had a kind of baptism (10:1–5). They were baptized when they passed through the waters of the Red Sea with Moses. And they had spiritual food and drink. God gave them manna and water in the desert. It was physical food, but it also embodied God's kindness to them and came to them through Christ (10:4).

But Paul's point is this: God judged these people. They are an example and a warning to us (10:6, 11). "Do not be idolaters as some of them were; as it is written, 'The people sat down to eat and drink and rose up to play'" (10:7). The problem is that they participated in idolatrous worship. And we can fall into temptation in the same way (10:11–13). "Therefore, my beloved," says Paul in verse 14, "flee from idolatry."

"But hang on a moment," you might say to Paul. "A moment ago you said that an idol is nothing, that there is only one real God, that eating meat does not make us worse off or better off. Make up your mind." But look at Paul's argument in verses 15–17:

> I speak as to sensible people; judge for yourselves what I say. The cup of blessing that we bless, is it not a participation [or "communion"] in the blood of Christ? The bread that we break, is it not a participation [or "communion"] in the body of Christ? Because there is one bread, we who are many are one body, for we all partake of the one bread.

Paul is drawing a parallel between pagan worship and Christian worship. The meat itself is not changed when offered to an idol. And it is the same with the bread and wine in Communion. They do not change their properties. They do not become magic—either for good or for ill. It's just meat. It's just bread. It's just wine.

But put this food in a *context*—the context of worship, of a meal, of a community, of faith—and everything changes. Context matters. In the context of the Christian community coming together in faith to worship Christ, eating bread and drinking become an act of participation or communion with Christ.

Communion is not just bread and wine; it is bread and wine with a liturgy (whether formal or informal), prayers, and Bible readings in the context of a community of faith. When we think about Christ's presence in Communion, we should not look at the bread and wine as objects in isolation. We need to lift our eyes and see the *whole* meal. The bread does not mystically change us, as if it is some kind of medicine. But neither is it merely a memory aid that touches our minds. It is part of a wider shared activity through which Christ is present by his Spirit.

In the same way, in the context of false worship and a false faith, eating meat becomes a demonic activity. "Consider the people of Israel," says Paul in verse 18. He is talking not about Israel in general here but about the specific occasions he has already mentioned in verses 7–10 when the Israelites participated in pagan worship.

> Consider the people of Israel: are not those who eat the sacrifices participants in the altar? What do I imply then? That food offered to idols is anything, or that an idol is anything? No, I imply that what pagans sacrifice they offer to demons and not to God. I do not want you to be participants with demons. (10:18–20)

An idol is nothing, Paul says in verse 19. Food offered to an idol is nothing. But in the context of pagan sacrifice, you participate with demons.

Paul's focus is on idolatry. But you see what this teaches about Communion. There is a sense in which, like the meat, the bread and wine are nothing. They do not change; they do not become magical. Christ is not made physically present in bread and wine. But the Lord's Supper is more than bread and wine. You can have bread and wine at home, and it means nothing. But bread and wine in the context of faith, of community, of worship is a different story. Here the bread and wine become an act of communion with Christ.

How does this happen? By the Holy Spirit. The Holy Spirit connects us to Christ. Through the Spirit's work "the ascended Lord is not everywhere . . . but he *is* everywhere accessible." says Douglas Farrow.[22] The Spirit collapses the gap between us and Christ, making Christ present among us. God "raised us up with [Christ]," says Ephesians 2:6, "and seated us with him in the heavenly places in Christ Jesus." It is not that the Spirit brings Christ down to us in some way so that he is physically present on earth again. Instead, we are lifted up to be with Christ. Thomas Cranmer says that "like eagles . . . we should fly up into heaven in our hearts, where that Lamb is resident at the right hand of his Father."[23] This is why Cranmer retained in the Communion liturgy of the Book of Common Prayer the call and response (known as the *Sursum Corda*):

> Lift up your hearts.
> We lift them up unto the Lord.

In Luke 10:21 we read: "In that same hour [Jesus] rejoiced in the Holy Spirit and said, 'I thank you, Father, Lord of heaven

---

22. Douglas Farrow, *Ascension and Ecclesia: On the Significance of the Doctrine of the Ascension for Ecclesiology and Christian Cosmology* (Edinburgh: T&T Clark, 1999), 178.

23. Thomas Cranmer, "Disputations at Oxford," in *The Works of Thomas Cranmer*, 1:398–99.

and earth, that you have hidden these things from the wise and understanding and revealed them to little children; yes, Father, for such was your gracious will.'" Notice that Jesus is full of joy "in the Holy Spirit." He praises God through the Spirit. The Holy Spirit unites the Father and Son in love. He is the connection between them. And the Spirit does the same work in us. He unites us to Jesus.

So Christ is really present when we take Communion. He may not be there physically, but he is there spiritually, and as Chad Van Dixhoorn notes, "spiritual does not mean artificial."[24] He is there to reassure us of his love, his protection, his covenant commitment. And *the bread and wine are physical signs of his spiritual presence*. The Westminster Confession says, "The body and blood of Christ are . . . as really, but spiritually, present to the faith of believers in that ordinance, as the elements themselves are to their outward senses" (29.7).

"But surely Christ is present with us by the Spirit all the time," you might say. "After all, that's what he promised before he ascended into heaven in Matthew 28:20." Yes. But *Christ in his kindness, knowing how frail we are, knowing how battered by life we can be, has given us bread and wine as physical signs of his presence*. Thomas Cranmer acknowledges that we cannot see spiritual life and nourishment:

> For this reason our Saviour Christ has not only set forth these things plainly in his holy word that we may hear them with our ears, but he has also ordained one visible sacrament of spiritual regeneration in water, and another visible sacrament of spiritual nourishment in bread and wine, with the intent, that as much as is possible for man, we may see Christ

---

24. Chad Van Dixhoorn, *Confessing the Faith: A Reader's Guide to the Westminster Confession of Faith* (Edinburgh: Banner of Truth, 2014), 397.

with our eyes, smell him with our nose, taste him with our mouths, touch him with our hands, and so perceive him with all our senses. Just as the word of God preached puts Christ into our ears, so in the same way these elements of water, bread, and wine, joined to God's word, put Christ in a sacramental way into our eyes, mouths, hands, and all our senses.[25]

Baptism is like a wedding. It is a covenant act, a relationship-making agreement, in which commitments are made. A couple may love one another. But feelings can go up and down. That is why marriage is so important. In a wedding two people bind themselves to one another in covenantal commitment. It provides a solid foundation to marriage. God has done the same with us. He has made a covenant. He has bound himself to us. And baptism symbolizes that commitment.

If baptism is like a wedding, then Communion is like an embrace. Communion is the reaffirmation of covenant love. Christ comes close to us to reassure us of his covenant love. He comes close to embrace us.

Consider a wife who has had an argument with her husband or has let him down in some way. What does she want? She wants him to take her in his arms and tell her that he loves her. She wants both the reassuring words *and* the physical touch of his embrace. Words without touch or touch without words could feel perfunctory, as if he were still withholding his affection. Christ is not withholding his affection for his bride, and so he graciously gives us both words and touch.

This is what gives such weight to Paul's argument in 1 Corinthians 10:21–22. In these verses the two parallel examples—pagan ceremonies and Christian Communion—collide: "You

---

25. Thomas Cranmer, "Defence of the True and Catholic Doctrine of the Sacrament, 1550," in *The Work of Thomas Cranmer*, ed. G. E. Duffield, The Courtenay Library of Reformation Classics 2 (Appleford: Sutton Courtenay, 1964), 70, modernized.

cannot drink the cup of the Lord and the cup of demons. You cannot partake of the table of the Lord and the table of demons. Shall we provoke the Lord to jealousy? Are we stronger than he?" Imagine a woman who has an intimate candle-lit meal with her husband and then leaves him to sleep with her lover. This is what happens, says Paul, if you come close to Christ in Communion and then leave him to sin. Do not be surprised if Jesus is jealous. Paul has already established in 1 Corinthians that we are united to Christ in a union akin to marriage so that our bodies are no longer our own (6:15–20). The eighteenth-century Scottish minister John Willison said, "The great God approaches very near to us, and we to Him; and yet it is to be deeply regretted that many who profess to believe this come to it with so little thought and preparation, and with so much indifference and carelessness of spirit."[26]

Paul talks about "the table of the Lord" in 1 Corinthians 10:21. We are hosted by Jesus. In Roman Catholicism the bread itself is effectively the host, because it hosts the physical presence of Christ. But in the New Testament it is not the bread that is the host (of Jesus) but Jesus who is the host (of us). So the host is not *on t*he table but *at* the table—it is, after all, the *Lord's* Table. For Jesus is present by the Holy Spirit, and he invites us to eat with him as an act of friendship and a sign of love. The people who serve are simply Jesus's way of getting the bread from the table into your hands.

I find this a really helpful way to think about what is taking place. When the plate or the bread is put in your hands, think quietly: "Jesus himself is giving me this bread. He is the host of this meal. This is his gift. This is a sign of his love. This is his

---

26. John Willison, *Sacramental Meditations and Advices* (1747), iii–vii, quoted in *Feasting with Christ: Meditations on the Lord's Supper*, ed. Joel Beeke and Paul Smalley (Darlington: Evangelical Press, 2012), 50–51.

embrace." Using the hands of the person serving you, Christ passes the bread and wine to you because he wants to have communion with you and because he wants to reassure you of his love. He offers you an invitation to taste and see that he is good. The seventeenth-century Dutch Reformer Wilhelmus à Brakel put it like this: "The Lord Jesus, the Bridegroom, comes in His love to them to have this Supper with them and to cause them to enjoy it together with Him. With love and delight He views them as they surround Him. It is there that the Holy Spirit is active, filling the soul with light, grace, and comforts."[27]

I was recently in a gift shop that had on display a map of North America showing all its "portkeys"—the magical portals of the Harry Potter novels. Spoiler alert: portkeys are fictional. But our connection with Christ at Communion is no fiction. And we could imagine a map plotting all the churches across the country, all the places were the Lord's Supper is celebrated. Each dot would represent a portal to heaven, for at the Lord's Supper earth and heaven intersect.

The Spirit connects us with Christ. He brings us into the presence of Christ. This is what you have to see in your imagination with the eyes of faith. By asking you to imagine, I do not mean pretend, as if this were not real. I mean see by faith the *spiritual reality* that is taking place. As we take Communion together, earth and heaven connect. Through the Spirit the Communion meal is a kind of portal to heaven. "The meeting place where the Lord's Supper is administered is at that moment none other than a portal of heaven," says à Brakel. "Heaven opens itself in such a place, and the rays of divine glory and grace descend to that place, filling it with the very presence of God."[28]

---

27. Wilhelmus à Brakel, *The Christian's Reasonable Service*, trans. Bartel Elshout, ed. Joel R. Beeke, vol. 2 (Grand Rapids, MI: Reformation Heritage, 1999), 573.

28. à Brakel, *The Christian's Reasonable Service*, 573.

Union and Communion

The seventeenth-century Puritan theologian John Owen writes, "Our communion with God consists in his communication of himself to us, with our return to him of that which he requires and accepts, flowing from that union which in Jesus Christ we have with him."[29] Owen distinguishes between communion with God, which is a two-way relationship to which we contribute, and union with God, which is a one-way relationship founded entirely on God's grace to us in Christ.

This is a really helpful distinction. Our day-to-day experience of God depends in part on our actions. When we respond to God's grace with faith and love, then we enjoy him more. We enjoy him more when we use the means of grace he has given, like prayer, Bible reading, worship, the life of the church, and so on. But this relationship is not something we achieve. It is founded entirely on God's grace in Christ. Our union with God comes down to Christ. We did not create it and we cannot break it. Our actions can affect our subjective experience of God but not the underlying objective reality of our relationship with God.

This distinction maps onto the sacraments:

- Baptism is the embodiment of our *union* with Christ.
- The Lord's Supper is the embodiment of our *communion* with Christ.

Baptism points me to my union with Christ. God has given us not just a word about union with Christ but also a physical sign and seal. Along with the preaching of the word, it is the chief means God has given us to enable us to understand who we are in Christ.

---

29. John Owen, *On Communion with God*, ed. William H. Goold, vol. 2 of *The Works of John Owen* (Edinburgh: Banner of Truth, 1966), 8–9, modernized.

Communion does not mean the same thing as baptism—otherwise we would be baptized repeatedly. Baptism is about *union* with Christ—it is a one-off, one-way act in which we are entirely passive (as we saw in chapter 1). Communion is about *communion* with Christ. Communion is an expression of the ongoing, two-way relationship we have with Christ because we have been united with him by grace.

We do not simply receive truth about Christ. We receive Christ himself, and in receiving Christ we receive all the treasures that are found in him. "To them God chose to make known how great among the Gentiles are the riches of the glory of this mystery, which is Christ in you, the hope of glory" (Col. 1:27). The Lord's Supper is the repeated renewal of this relationship in which we receive in Christ the glorious riches of God.

So the Lord's Supper is not simply "a means of grace." It is a means of *communion*. This is the place where we come to commune with Christ, to experience afresh the fruit of our union with him. When we are weary, doubting, fearful, guilt ridden, frustrated, proud, anxious, we come to the bread and wine. We receive them as a sign of our union with Christ and a means of our communion with him. In this way he nourishes our souls.

My Hand in His Hand, My Life in His Life

Consider this reflection on bereavement:[30]

> My deepest regret [is] that I did not hold her hand more.
>
> It's not, of course, that I never held her hand. It is likely, however, that I didn't as often as she would have liked. Holding her hand communicates to her in a simple yet profound way that we are connected. Taking her hand tells her, "I am

---

30. R. C. Sproul Jr., "Husbands, Hold Your Wife's Hand," originally posted at http://www.ligonier.org/blog, October 4, 2014, now available through http://web.archive.org. Quoted by permission.

grateful that we are one flesh." Taking her hand tells me, "This is bone of my bone, flesh of my flesh." It is a liturgy, an ordinary habit of remembrance to see more clearly the extraordinary reality of two being made one. It would have, even in the midst of a disagreement, or moments of struggle, communicated, "We're going to go through this together. I will not let go."

. . . Holding her hand more would have communicated to us both my own calling to lead her, and our home. Hand holding is a way to say both, "You are safe with me" and "Follow me into the adventure." It would have reminded me that there is no abdicating, no shirking, no flinching in the face of responsibility. And as I lead it would be a constant anchor, a reminder that I lead not for my sake, but for hers.

Holding her hand more also would have spoken with clarity to the watching world. It would have said, "There's a man who loves his wife." It saddens me that so many only learn this after their wife is gone. Perhaps most of all, however, I wish I had held her hand more so that I could still feel it more clearly. I wish it had been such a constant habit that even now my hand would form into a hand-holding shape each time I get in the car. I wish I could fall asleep feeling her hand in mine.

I know all this, happily, because I did hold her hand. I received all the blessings I describe above. I just wish I had received them more. It cost nothing, and bears dividends even to this day. If, for you, it's not too late, make the investment. Hold her hand, every chance you get. You won't regret it.

I want to suggest that this is a powerful picture of the way the Lord's Supper works. It is a picture of the Lord's Supper because, like holding hands, the Lord's Supper is a physical act that has no intrinsic power but carries tremendous power in a covenantal context. And it is a picture of the Lord's Supper because, like holding hands, the Lord's Supper is the embodiment of a covenantal relationship. So, with all due apologies, let me rewrite these words, making them about Communion. In doing so, we need to invert some of the statements because we are the bride and Christ is the husband.

> My deepest regret is that I have not partaken of Communion more—or, rather, that I have not given it the significance it deserves.
>
> It's not, of course, that I never take Communion. It is likely, however, that I don't as often as Christ would like me to. Communion communicates in a simple yet profound way that we are connected. In Communion, Christ tells me, "I am glad that we are one flesh." In Communion, Christ says to me, "You are bone of my bone, flesh of my flesh." It is a liturgy, an ordinary habit of remembrance, by which I see more clearly the extraordinary reality of two being made one. It is a means by which, even in the midst of a disagreement, or moments of struggle, Christ communicates to me: "We're going to go through this together. I will not let go."
>
> It also communicates to me his calling to lead me. Communion is a way for him to say both "You are safe with me" and "Follow me into the adventure." It reminds me that he will not abdicate, shirk, or flinch in the face of responsibility. And as he leads me, Communion is a constant anchor, a reminder that he leads not for his benefit but for mine.
>
> Taking Communion more would also speak with clarity to the watching world. It would say, "There's a person who loves the Savior."
>
> Perhaps most of all, however, I wish I had taken Communion more so that I would feel the gospel more clearly. I wish it had been such a constant habit that even now my life would form into a gospel shape throughout the day. I wish I could fall asleep feeling my life in his life.

I know all this, happily, because I have taken Communion. I have received all the blessings I describe above. I just wish I had received them more. It costs nothing, and bears dividends even to this day. If, for you, it's not too late, make the investment. Take Communion, receive it with meaning, every chance you get. You won't regret it.

This link between couples holding hands and Communion is important for another reason. This account of a husband's relationship with his wife may have evoked regret or longing in some readers. You want the kind of marital relationship the author describes, and you are frustrated that you do not enjoy it. And then Christians say, "But you have Christ." And you know that's true, and you know he should be enough. But where is the holding of hands? Where is the touch? Where is the embodied relationship? Whether we are married or single, we want our relationship with Christ to be real and felt.

So let's go back to our single woman with whom we began this chapter, the woman walking back to an empty home, longing for the physical touch of a man. How does she find satisfaction in Christ? When temptation comes, what does knowing Christ taste like?

The answer is *red wine*. Red wine in the context of faith and community. The Lord's Supper is the physical expression of our covenant relationship with Christ. The Lord's Supper is something we touch and taste. And, in the words and prayers that surround it, it is something we hear. We hear Christ's word to us in the promises of the gospel, and we receive those promises in bread and wine. Think of the bread and wine as a lover's touch. It is as much a physical sign of Christ's love to you as holding his hand. Communion is the embrace of Christ.

4

ENACTED MEMORY

We all need reminders. We stick Post-it notes on the fridge, scribble words on our hands in ballpoint pen, even perhaps tie knots in the corners of handkerchiefs. My home is littered with lists my wife has written on scraps of paper. They're her way of ordering her life.

We sometimes talk of people "forgetting themselves" when they fail to act in a way befitting their roles. Once when I was playing soccer for my school team, and my sports teacher was supposed to be refereeing the match with all due impartiality, he "forgot" himself. In his frustration with us, he forgot his role as a referee and started acting like a coach, barking out instructions.

But remembering matters not just because appointments might be missed, tasks left undone, or roles forgotten. Many of our towns have war memorials or statues to commemorate those who gave their lives in the two world wars. Often they list the people from the local area who died or served during the war. A memorial is a particular kind of reminder, a reminder in permanent, physical form. We create these reminders because we do not want to fail in our obligation to honor the dead. We want to maintain their legacy.

Remembering Involves Reliving the Story

Remembering is important. Our shared stories give us our identity and shape the way we live. That is true of any family, community, or nation. And it is especially true for God's people. Psalm 105 begins:

> Oh *give thanks* to the LORD; *call* upon his name;
>> *make known* his deeds among the peoples!
> *Sing* to him, *sing* praises to him;
>> *tell* of all his wondrous works!
> *Glory* in his holy name;
>> let the hearts of those who *seek* the LORD rejoice!
> *Seek* the LORD and his strength;
>> *seek* his presence continually! (vv. 1–4)

There are ten commands in these verses (shown here in italics) encompassing worship, evangelism, allegiance, trust, communion—all of the Christian life is here. But how are we to fulfill these commands? The answer is through one final command: *Remember*. The psalmist continues:

> *Remember* the wondrous works that he has done,
>> his miracles, and the judgments he uttered,
> O offspring of Abraham, his servant,
>> children of Jacob, his chosen ones!
> He is the LORD our God;
>> his judgments are in all the earth. (vv. 5–7)

What we do for God flows out of what he has done to us. The calls to praise and proclaim in verse 1 flow from "the wondrous works that he has done" in verse 5.

Obedience falters when memory fails.

The prophet Micah brings a lawsuit on behalf of God against God's people. "The LORD has an indictment against his people," he says (Mic. 6:2). The problem is that the people regard God's rule as a burden. What is God's exhortation? Remember.

> O my people, remember . . .
> what happened from Shittim to Gilgal,
> > that you may know the righteous acts of the LORD.
> > (Mic. 6:5)

If they will only remember all that God has done for them, then they will gladly live as his people without grumbling.

The apostle Peter makes the same point. "His divine power has granted to us all things that pertain to life and godliness," he tells his readers. Peter starts with what God has said and done, then adds, "by which he has granted to us his precious and very great promises" (2 Pet. 1:3–4). Only then does he exhort us to "make every effort" to add to our faith goodness, knowledge, self-control, perseverance, godliness, mutual affection, and love (2 Pet. 1:5–7). What is the problem when people do not grow in these virtues? Memory failure! "For whoever lacks these qualities," says Peter, "is so nearsighted that he is blind, having forgotten that he was cleansed from his former sins" (2 Pet. 1:9). What is the solution? Reminders. "Therefore I intend always to remind you of these qualities," he says. "I think it right . . . to stir you up by way of reminder. . . . And I will make every effort so that after my departure you may be able at any time to recall these things" (2 Pet. 1:12–15) Three times Peter describes his task as reminding God's people.

The primary way we are to encourage, counsel, and exhort one another is through reminding one another of the gospel. Of course, there are times when Christians, especially new Christians, must be taught truths they did not previously know. But most of the time what we need to hear is "the old, old story of Jesus and his love."[1] This is what preachers must offer in their preaching, counselors must offer in their counsel, and friends must offer in their conversations. And this is what Christ offers in the Lord's Supper.

We need reminders. And so throughout the Bible story God gives his people reminders. Sometimes those reminders take the form of physical memorials. When God parted the Jordan River so his people could enter the promised land, he told them to take twelve stones from the river bed to create "a sign among you . . . a memorial forever" (Josh. 4:6–7). When God delivered Israel from the Philistines, "Samuel took a stone and set it up between Mizpah and Shen and called its name Ebenezer; for he said, 'Till now the Lord has helped us'" (1 Sam. 7:12).

Sometimes those reminders take the form of rites or rituals. We have already seen in chapter 2 how God instituted the Passover festival to remind the people of the exodus. "This day shall be for you a memorial day, and you shall keep it as a feast to the Lord; throughout your generations, as a statute forever, you shall keep it as a feast" (Ex. 12:14). It was not a memorial that the people would *see*; it was a memorial that people would do—a memorial that takes the form of a meal.

God even wove reminders into the fabric of the clothing of the Israelites by telling them to add tassels to the corners of their garments: "And it shall be a tassel for you to look at and remember all the commandments of the Lord, to do them, not to follow after your own heart and your own eyes, which you are inclined to whore after" (Num. 15:39).

It may be that you want to create your own memorials—physical objects or family rituals—that remind you of God's

---

1. From the hymn by Katherine Hankey, "Tell Me the Old, Old Story of Jesus and His Love" (1866).

work in your life. You might write a note in your Bible or use festivals like New Year's Day or Thanksgiving to remember God's work in your life. But the memorials that are given collectively to new covenant believers are baptism and Communion.

Some people have dramatic conversion stories. They can name the day, even the moment, when they passed from death to life. But for many of us it felt more gradual and we cannot name the day. Perhaps you grew up in a Christian home and have always believed; perhaps it felt like the truth of the gospel dawned on you over a period of time. But for all us God's promise of salvation took physical form in our baptism. Baptism marks a moment we can look back to—a moment we can remember when God's grace came to us in the form of a promise to which we can now respond with faith.

Likewise, Communion is a regular reminder of all that God has done for us in Christ. Communion is more than a memorial. Remembering is not the only thing that is happening, and in fact the call to remember is not mentioned in Matthew and Mark's account of the Last Supper. Nevertheless, Communion is certainly *not less than a memorial*. Remembering is a central element in the Lord's Supper. After all, Jesus said, "Do this in *remembrance* of me" (Luke 22:19; 1 Cor. 11:24–25). Perhaps it should have been enough for God simply to tell us what he had done. Perhaps it should be enough for us simply to exhort one another to remember God's grace. *But God in his kindness, knowing how frail we are, knowing how battered by life we can be, also gives us physical reminders of his grace in water, bread, and wine.*

Therefore, Remembering Leads to Identity Formation

Communion is not simply an act through which we recall the death of Christ. The act of remembering *changes* those involved. It leads to identity formation. It allows the past to shape the present. It enrolls us in the story. Just as the Lord's Supper connects earth and heaven through Spirit-enabled communion, so it also connects past and present through Spirit-empowered remembrance.

The Gettysburg Address is routinely reenacted in schools across the United States. What is the effect of this practice? It has shaped generation after generation of young Americans, giving them a sense of national identity and reinforcing values of freedom and democracy. It matters, too, that this speech is not merely learned at home but publicly enacted. Those in the room are bound together by what happens on the stage.

Remembering shapes the people of God in a similar way. At the end of his life, King David looked back over the way God had delivered him from danger and exalted him to the throne. That reflection on his life took the form of a psalm of praise to the Lord, "my rock and my fortress and my deliverer." David begins by describing how "the earth reeled and rocked" as the Lord came down to him. "The LORD thundered from heaven," and "the channels of the sea were seen." "He drew me out of many waters," says David (2 Sam. 22:2, 8, 14, 16, 17). He is describing the exodus—the rescue of God's people through the Red Sea—and the encounter with God at Mount Sinai. The language of 2 Samuel 22:8–15 is full of echoes of Exodus 19:16, 18, and 20:18, 21. Except, of course, that the exodus did not take place during David's lifetime—it took place many years before. The most formative moment of David's life did not occur during his lifetime!

The point is that David was part of the people who were saved through the exodus. His existence depended on that moment. The nation over which he ruled was born through that event. God's grace toward David was founded on that covenant. It was as if all the future generations of Israel had passed through the Sea with Moses. The Jewish *Haggadah*, the text read at each celebration of the Passover, says that "in every generation, each individual is bound to regard himself as if he personally had gone forth from Egypt."[2]

In a similar way, we have passed through judgment with Jesus. Jesus died, was buried, and rose again. And our baptism brings those past events into our present. We physically reenact the drama of the story. United with Christ, we are "buried" under the water (through whatever mode of baptism is used), before rising again out of the water to a new life—a point Paul makes in Romans 6:3–4. We reenact the story in baptism not just to remember it but also to make it our own.

Communion, too, brings the past event of Christ's death into the present. We remember, but by remembering we make the benefits of his death our own. The past becomes a present reality, and we are assured of the forgiveness of our sins.

When Moses passed on God's instructions for the Passover memorial meal, he added this: "And when your children say to you, 'What do you mean by this service?' you shall say, 'It is the sacrifice of the LORD's Passover, for he passed over the houses of the people of Israel in Egypt, when he struck the Egyptians but spared our houses'" (Ex. 12:26–27). His assistant Joshua must have taken note of this, for when he passed on God's instructions to create a memorial of the parting of the river Jordan with twelve stones, he said much the same thing: "When your children ask in time to come, 'What do those stones mean to you?' then you shall tell them that the waters of the Jordan were cut off before the ark of the covenant of the LORD'" (Josh. 4:6–7).

The physical memorial worked together with the spoken word to point future generations to the story. In this way, they

---

2. Quoted in David Grossman, "The Second Book of Moses, Called Exodus," in *Revelations: Personal Responses to the Books of the Bible* (Edinburgh: Canongate, 2005), 55.

would learn who God is and who they are. Remembering in this way was intended to shape their identity. It would enroll them into the story so that the story became their own.

Imagine a mother looking at a photo album with a child. "And there's you with your uncle Albert." "There's your dad playing football." This is not simply an act of recall. It is an act of enrollment. It is shaping the identity of the children. It is placing them in a wider family and a larger story. And notice that this involves physical objects, in this case photographs. But it could be other objects: old toys, significant places, family heirlooms, favorite foods. Objects that have no meaning in and of themselves are able to impart meaning and identity in the context of relationships and stories. It is the same for us with water, bread, and wine.

Moses says future generations are to talk about how God "spared *our* houses" (Ex. 12:27). By reenacting the Passover story, they would be able to speak of *our* houses and *our* deliverance. In the same way, when we reenact the story of the cross in the Lord's Supper, it becomes our story and our identity. We have died with Christ, and we will rise with him.

Remembering Involves Fulfilling the Covenant

Let's return to Psalm 105. We have seen how verses 5–7 are an exhortation to remember what God has done, an exhortation that in part finds fulfillment in the Lord's Supper. But notice how the psalm continues:

> He remembers his covenant forever,
> > the word that he commanded, for a thousand
> > > generations,
> the covenant that he made with Abraham,
> > his sworn promise to Isaac. (vv. 8–9)

Having exhorted us to remember, the psalmist now tells us that *God* remembers. Now, that should come as something of a surprise. Was God's remembering ever in doubt? Is he known for memory lapses? The answer is no. He is the God who knows all things. After all, he is the eternal God who exists outside of time. He has no past, present, and future. He is the great "I AM." Every moment is present to him.

The key to making sense of God's remembering is to notice the central thrust of these verses in the words "covenant," "word," "covenant," and "sworn promise" in successive lines. God is not simply recalling pieces of information. He is remembering his covenant promises. *In the Bible "remembering" is a covenantal term.*

"Remembering" can describe mental recall—a forgotten fact comes to mind. When Joseph is in prison, he interprets the dream of Pharaoh's cupbearer. Then Joseph adds: "Only remember me, when it is well with you, and please do me the kindness to mention me to Pharaoh, and so get me out of this house. . . . Yet the chief cupbearer did not remember Joseph, but forgot him" (Gen. 40:14, 23). Only when Pharaoh himself has a dream does the cupbearer recall his commitment to Joseph. "Then the chief cupbearer said to Pharaoh, 'I remember my offenses today'" (Gen. 41:9). He tells Pharaoh about Joseph's ability to interpret dreams, and the rest is history.

But just as often—and always when used in relation to God— "remembering" means acting to keep covenant promises. (Even in the story of Joseph and the cupbearer, the cupbearer's mental recall leads him to keep his promise to Joseph.) The words "he remembers his covenant forever" in Psalm 105:8 mean God is continually faithful to his covenant promises—he always does what he has said he will do. When the Bible says God remembers his covenant, it means he is about to keep his promises.

It is not that the promise had previously slipped his mind and now he has recalled it. Rather, the time has come for God to act according to his previous commitments.

This kind of "remembering" is not such a strange idea for us. It is actually a way of talking with which we are already familiar. Suppose I make a contract with you in which I commit to give you a hundred dollars on your next birthday. When the day arrives, you turn up at my house with the contract in your hand, pointing to my signature at the bottom. "Remember this?" you say. You do not mean, "Do you remember that day when we both went to a lawyer's office and the sun was shining? You were wearing your red sweater and the lawyer made that joke about you looking like Father Christmas." No, that is not what you mean. What you mean when you say "Remember this?" is "Give me the money!" It is time for me to act in line with the covenant I made.

Or consider Paul's account of what the Jerusalem apostles said to him when they met together: "Only, they asked us to remember the poor, the very thing I was eager to do" (Gal. 2:10). What does this mean? If remembering were just mental recall, then all Paul would have been urged to do was to bring the poor to mind from time to time. If that were all remembering involved, then he would have fulfilled this exhortation by occasionally saying to himself, "There are poor people in the world—how sad." But of course the apostles were actually urging Paul *to act* to meet the needs of the poor—something he gladly did through his collection of money for the poor in Jerusalem. "Remembering" in Galatians 2:10 is not simply a mental exercise; it describes practical action. It means fulfilling a commitment.

This is what it means for God to remember: he is acting to fulfill his covenant commitments. When the Israelites cry out in their slavery, we read, "God heard their groaning, and God remembered his covenant with Abraham, with Isaac, and with

Jacob" (Ex. 2:24). As a result, he comes down to call Moses to lead the people to freedom (Ex. 3:8). God had not forgotten them. He was waiting for the moment of fulfillment to come, and now that time has come and he is about to act.

In Psalm 105, as we have seen, the psalmist exhorts us to "remember the wondrous works that he has done" (v. 5). This is then followed by a long section in which he describes all the things God has done for his people—rescuing them from famine through Joseph (vv. 12–22); redeeming them from slavery through the plagues on Egypt (vv. 23–38); providing for them in the wilderness (vv. 39–41). But this central description of God's actions begins and ends with an account of God remembering:

> He remembers his covenant forever,
>> the word that he commanded, for a thousand
>>> generations,
> the covenant that he made with Abraham,
>> his sworn promise to Isaac. (vv. 8–9)

> For he remembered his holy promise,
>> and Abraham, his servant. (vv. 42)

All that God has done, he has done because he "remembered"—in the sense of "kept" or "fulfilled"—his covenant promises. And this is what we are to remember: history shows that God is both *able* to keep his covenant promises and *willing* to keep his covenant promises. We are to remember that God remembers.

So, in a covenantal context, remembering is not simply an act of looking back. It is something that happens in the present: it is an act of covenant fulfillment or renewal.

Here is the remarkable thing. Not only does God remember his covenant promises in this way; he also builds in memorials or memory aids to ensure that he remembers.

We often talk about a rainbow being a reminder to us of God's promise never again to flood the earth. But that is not what the text of Genesis says.

> And God said, "This is the sign of the covenant that I make between me and you and every living creature that is with you, for all future generations: I have set my bow in the cloud, and it shall be a sign of the covenant between me and the earth. When I bring clouds over the earth and the bow is seen in the clouds, I will remember my covenant that is between me and you and every living creature of all flesh. And the waters shall never again become a flood to destroy all flesh. When the bow is in the clouds, I will see it and remember the everlasting covenant between God and every living creature of all flesh that is on the earth." (9:12–16)

The rainbow is a covenant sign. But twice God says that *he* is the one who will see it and remember his covenant promise. There is no mention of Noah being comforted by the sight of the rainbow (though no doubt he was). The covenant sign is for God's benefit. It is a memory aid for God.

We find the same pattern again when God tells the Israelites to make two trumpets of silver (Num. 10:1–10). While the people are in the wilderness, these trumpets call them to gather and signal when they are to break camp. But the trumpets will have different uses when the people of Israel live in the promised land.

First, the trumpets are to be sounded when Israel goes into battle. But this is not, as we might imagine, a signal to the people to attack. Instead, it is a signal to the Lord to remember: "... that you may be remembered before the LORD your God, and you shall be saved from your enemies" (10:9). It is not, of course, that God's people have somehow slipped his mind. Instead, this is an evocation to God—a kind of embodied prayer—to act in line with his covenant promises and so protect his people.

The second time the trumpets are used is when sacrifices are made at Israel's festivals. And, again, their purpose is to call on God to remember: "They shall be a reminder of you before your God" (10:10). The memorial is directed toward God for the sake of the people. Again, it is a kind of prayer in which the people call on God to act in line with his covenant promises and so forgive their sins.

The point is that in all these cases there is a call to remember directed toward God, which is intended to evoke the covenant and bring about real change in the present. These are not acts of mere recollection; they are acts of covenant application.

Why does the eternal, all-knowing God set up for himself "memorials" or memory aids? It cannot be that he needs his memory jogged. I suspect instead the answer is that these memorials are created or performed to strengthen *our* faith. It ought to be enough for us to hear God's promise, but the writer of Hebrews says, "He guaranteed it with an oath" for our benefit so we can be doubly sure, "as a sure and steadfast anchor of the soul" (Heb. 6:17, 19). In a similar way, the memorials are given to anchor our faith. God does not need memorials, but we do. When life is tough, it is all too easy for us to feel forgotten by God. *So God in his kindness, knowing how frail we are, knowing how battered by life we can be, has put in place memorials—including water, bread, and wine—so we never need feel forgotten by him.* We are reminded that he remembers.

Therefore, Remembering Leads to Covenant Renewal

Remembering as a covenantal act has big implications for the way we view the remembrance of Christ's death in the Lord's Supper. For Jesus's call to "do this in remembrance of me" comes smack-dab in a covenantal context. His very next words are "This cup that is poured out for you is the new covenant in my blood" (Luke 22:19–20).

On the night before he died, Jesus made a covenant with his people. He committed himself to the forgiveness of their sins. "This is my blood of the covenant, which is poured out for many for the forgiveness of sins" (Matt. 26:28). The covenant agreement was sealed by drinking a shared cup of wine. That was like his signature at the bottom of the contract or like shaking hands on the deal.

The next day, Jesus fulfilled the requirements of the covenant by shedding his blood on the cross. The wine is called the "blood of the covenant" because it is a picture of the way God delivered on his covenant promise, that is, through the shed blood of his Son. We can be forgiven, and therefore God can be true to his covenant, because Jesus died on the cross, bearing the penalty our sin deserves.

So, when we celebrate Communion "in remembrance" of Jesus, we are not simply recalling the past. We are calling on God to act in keeping with his covenant promises. We are asking him to forgive our sins through the blood of Jesus. When we remember this moment in the Lord's Supper, it is as if we were there at the Last Supper. Jesus renews the covenant with us. He signs it with us as we drink the wine. It is as if we are shaking hands on his covenant promise afresh. Thomas Cranmer comments:

> In this sacrament (if it is rightly received with true faith) we are assured that our sins are forgiven, and the league of peace and the testament [or "covenant"] of God is confirmed between him and us. Whoever with true faith eats Christ's flesh and drinks his blood has everlasting life by

him. What can be more joyful, more pleasant, or more comforting to us that to feel this in our hearts as we receive of the Lord's Supper?[3]

But it is not just God's covenant commitments that are remembered in the Lord's Supper. So are ours. A covenant is a relationship-forming agreement. God has entered into a covenant relationship with his people. God agrees to be our God and we agree to be his people. The relationship begins when we are born again as children of God and respond to the gospel with faith. Our entry into that covenant relationship is then marked by baptism. Baptism is the "signature" on the agreement. The Puritan Thomas Manton explains:

> Now the covenant mutually binds us. God binds himself to
> give grace to us, and we bind ourselves to live for God.... So
> sacraments on God's part are signs and seals of the promise
> of grace; on our part, they are an obligation to obedience.
> God binds himself to be our God, and we bind ourselves to
> be his people.[4]

The Lord's Supper is the regular renewal or ratification of the agreement. It expresses God's commitment to us—that, as we have seen, is its primary purpose. But it *also* expresses our commitment to him. "In every repetition of communion," says Stephen Charnock, "by presenting the sacrament God confirms his resolution to stick to his covenant; and by eating it the receiver commits himself to keep close to the condition of faith."[5]

3. Thomas Cranmer, "Defence of the True and Catholic Doctrine of the Sacrament, 1550," in *The Work of Thomas Cranmer*, ed. G. E. Duffield, The Courtenay Library of Reformation Classics 2 (Appleford: Sutton Courtenay, 1964), 75–76, modernized.

4. Thomas Manton, "A Sermon on the Ends of the Sacrament," in *The Complete Works of Thomas Manton* (London: James Nisbet, 1873), 493.

5. Stephen Charnock, "A Discourse upon the Goodness of God," in *The Complete Works of Stephen Charnock*, vol. 2 (Edinburgh: James Nichol, 1864), 342–43, word order changed for clarity.

Matthew Henry reminds us of this in his prayer of preparation for the Lord's Supper: "Thou hast taken me into covenant with thee, for I am a baptized Christian, set apart for thee and sealed to be thine; thou hast laid me, and I have also laid myself, under all possible obligations to love thee and serve thee and live to thee."[6]

The biblical scholar Joachim Jeremias argued that at Communion the remembering is done by God, not by the disciples. What is remembered is clearly Jesus and his death, since Jesus says, "Do this in remembrance *of me*." But Jeremias maintained that the reminder of Christ's finished work is directed toward God. "Something is brought before God," he said, "that God may remember."[7] The fact that many Old Testament memorials were, as we have seen, directed toward God supports this conclusion.

But there are good reasons for thinking the remembrance in Communion is directed (or also directed) toward us as we participate. First, the context of Luke's account of the Last Supper is the Passover meal (which Luke repeatedly highlights), and the Passover was specifically described as a memorial "between your eyes," that is, a memorial directed toward the people (Ex. 13:9). Second, in 1 Corinthians 11:24–25, Paul's description of the Lord's Supper as a remembrance is a remedy for its misuse in Corinth, where some Christians were *forgetting* key aspects of the death of Christ. They are the ones who are being urged to recall their identity in Christ and the pattern of the cross.

We enter the visible church through baptism, and we express our ongoing belonging to the church through Communion. So when we participate in Communion, we are renewing our cove-

---

6. Matthew Henry, "Before Partaking of the Lord's Supper," in *Pray the Bible: An Online Edition of Matthew Henry's "A Method of Prayer,"* ed. Ligon Duncan with William McMillan, http://www.matthewhenry.org/read/esv-corporate/chapter-nine/?page=9#.W3LgJC 3Mwo8.

7. Joachim Jeremias, *Eucharistic Words of Jesus* (London: SCM, 1966), 248; for his full argument, see 237–55.

nant commitment to Christ and his people. "The Lord's Supper," says the Puritan Edmund Calamy, "implies a covenant transaction between God and us and supposes a renewal of our vows to be the Lord's [people]."[8] Elsewhere Calamy says, "The express renewal of the Christian vow, every time we come to the Supper of our Lord will help us more effectively to reap the benefits of that holy ordinance."[9] The temptations of the world and the flesh are continually pulling at us to deviate from the path of holiness. But renewing our commitment to Christ at the Supper, says Calamy, "will much fix and awe our slippery hearts."[10]

Every Lord's Supper is a covenant-renewal ceremony in this way. But it might be helpful to have an annual Communion service in which covenant renewal is the main focus, a chance to recommit to be members of the church.

We remember our covenant commitments, not just recalling that they exist but recommitting ourselves to keep those commitments. Think what commitment to Christ involves:

- A radical repudiation of sin, selfishness, self-reliance, and pride
- A commitment to look to Christ, and Christ alone, for salvation from sin and death
- A commitment to find our ultimate identity and fulfillment in Christ
- A commitment to deny ourselves, take up our cross, and follow him
- A commitment to obey his every command
- A commitment to extend his reign through the proclamation of the gospel

8. Edmund Calamy, "The Lord's Supper Is a Federal Ordinance," in *The Puritans on the Lord's Supper*, ed. Don Kistler (Morgan, PA: Soli Deo Gloria, 1997), 24.

9. Edmund Calamy, "The Express Renewal of Our Covenant Vows," in Kistler, *The Puritans on the Lord's Supper*, 38.

10. Calamy, "The Express Renewal," 39.

And think, too, what commitment to Christ's people involves:

- A commitment to attend regularly
- A commitment to pray faithfully
- A commitment to serve fully
- A commitment to give sacrificially
- A commitment to participate in the church's mission
- A commitment to disciple others, to be discipled, and (if necessary) to be disciplined

This is what we are signing up for when we take Communion. Except we do not literally "sign up." Instead, we "eat up" and "drink up," making our covenant commitments by participating in the Lord's Supper together as an act of covenant renewal. It is not something to be done lightly. There should be a weight to what takes place. These are the commitments we make to Christ, and these are the commitments we make to one another.

5

A BAPTIZED LIFE

Paul often points people back to their baptism (as we saw in the introduction under "Thought Experiment 2"). He expects it to shape their behavior and attitudes. This is not something I have been used to doing. For many of us baptism is an event that merely belongs in the past. It does not impinge on the present. How should baptism and Communion shape our lives? How do they help us walk as disciples of Jesus?

Baptism Changes Our Status

In a television documentary on the medieval statesman William the Marshal, Thomas Asbridge says:

> For me one of the most evocative moments from William's life is that instance when he is created as a knight. But the most important part of that occasion for him, as it is for all other knights, is the moment when the sword is girded to his side. . . . It's a moment of transformation when they go from being one type of human being to another.[1]

---

1. Thomas Asbridge, *The Greatest Knight: William the Marshal*, BBC Two, broadcast on November 1, 2014.

Here is an act that has no intrinsic magic. It is, in one sense, merely a symbol. But symbolic acts can be hugely significant if and when they are performed in certain contexts. Indeed, they can be transforming. William would have girded a sword to his side day after day. But on this occasion it was literally life-changing, because it was part of a symbolic ceremony in a particular social and cultural context. It took on a significance that went beyond the bare act itself. As Asbridge says, "It's a moment of transformation when they go from being one type of human being to another."

A man holds up his hand and repeats some words. And in that moment he goes from being an ordinary citizen to being the president of the United States. He (at least so far it has always been a "he") repeats words read to him by the person officiating, usually the chief justice. So they both say the same words, but only one of them becomes the president. The words have no intrinsic transforming power. If you do not believe me, have a go now. Repeat the following words and see if you become the most powerful person in the world: "I do solemnly swear that I will faithfully execute the Office of President of the United States, and will to the best of my ability, preserve, protect and defend the Constitution of the United States." The words have no power in themselves. They are not a magic spell. But said by the right person in the right social context, they transform that person into something new, someone with enormous power. They do not simply *describe* reality. They actually *change* reality. The day before, he merely had opinions and intentions. The day after, he can send the world's largest army into battle.

Symbolic acts can be very powerful.

On July 22, 1989, I said the words "I do," and a woman placed a ring on my finger. In that moment my status changed decisively and permanently. I become a husband. What did our wedding ceremony achieve? It did not create love between two people. But it did change our relationship. It brought us into a *covenant* relationship. We were now bound together by promises. It changed our status. I became a married man. Indeed, that change is so decisive that I cannot undo it. I may one day become a widower. In theory I could become a divorcé. But I can never again be single.

Like the presidential oath, the words and the ring are not in themselves intrinsically powerful. A single person could put a ring on his or her finger and shout "I do." But that in itself would not change the person's status. The words have power only in a ritual and social context. In the context of ceremony and community, words and symbols can be life-changing.

This is true of baptism and Communion. The water, bread, and wine are just water, bread, and wine. They have no intrinsic power. We do not believe, as Catholics do, in baptismal regeneration, in which the very act of baptism saves the person and makes the recipient a Christian. Baptism is "just" a symbolic act. But symbolic acts can be very powerful. These "mere" signs can change reality when they take place in the context of the community of faith. They are "just" symbols. But symbols have power. They can transform our status.

We know this not only from presidential oaths and marriage ceremonies. We know this from the Bible story. There was nothing intrinsically magical about the fruit of the tree of the knowledge of good and evil. It was not somehow spiritually poisonous. It was a symbol—a symbol of trust in God. But that symbol was powerful, so powerful that it brought ruin to humanity. The same is true of circumcision. Circumcision was common in the ancient world. Other nations circumcised their children, yet their children did not become part of God's people.

But circumcision was status-changing within the context created by God's covenant promises.

Baptism is a symbolic act. But it is a symbolic act that changes your status.

At the end of his ministry on earth, Jesus told his disciples: "All authority in heaven and on earth has been given to me. Go therefore and make disciples of all nations, baptizing them in the name of the Father and of the Son and of the Holy Spirit, teaching them to observe all that I have commanded you" (Matt. 28:18–20). We are baptized into the name of the Father, the Son, and the Holy Spirit. Baptism is a naming ceremony. We now carry the name of the Father, the Son and the Holy Spirit. Our relationship with God does not begin at baptism, but baptism is when it is made public. We are adopted by God the Father.

Or think of baptism as being like a wedding. Marriage is more than a wedding. But a wedding is important. It signals your change of status. You may not feel different. But your identity has changed completely. It is not that you need to live like a married person so you become more married. It is the other way around: you get married so you can live as a married person. Nor can you be half married and half single. You are completely married.

It is the same with baptism. Baptism changes your status. It is not that you need to live like a Christian so you become more Christian. Baptism declares that you are in Christ. You have died with him and risen with him.

God himself is active in the covenant of marriage. We might think that what ties people together in marriage are the vows they make. But there is a bigger picture. Jesus says: "'Therefore a man shall leave his father and mother and hold fast to his wife, and the two shall become one flesh.' So they are no longer two but one flesh. What therefore God has joined together, let not man separate" (Mark 10:7–9). What joins them together is not simply their choices or even the act of sex. It is God who joins them together through their covenant commitments. Every marriage really is "a match made in heaven." The same is true of the covenant of baptism. It might look like the persons being baptized become part of the church through the vows they make or the vows made on their behalf. But each is a match made in heaven. When the covenant-making act of baptism is combined with faith, then God himself is uniting us with Christ and his people.

Baptism and Communion are symbolic acts that change reality because they are *covenantal*. A covenant is a bit like a contract. Promises are made and commitments are given. It is a formal act. But a covenant is more than a contract or a particular type of contract. Covenants create or change the relationship of those involved. Marriage is a contract that creates a new type of relationship between a man and a woman. Covenants, we could say, are relational contracts. Baptism declares and affirms the covenant or contract that God makes with Christians. And Jesus describes the wine as "the new covenant in my blood" (Luke 22:20). Baptism is the act by which the covenant is affirmed, and Communion is the act by which the covenant is *re*affirmed. So baptism and Communion do not create a relationship with God, but they do change its nature. They make it a covenantal relationship. Asking why we should get baptized is like asking a couple why they want a wedding.

Tomb and Womb

This is what it means to live "a baptized life": it means we are people whose status has radically changed. We have become Christ's. We have a new identity. Baptism is a naming ceremony, and as a result we are now the children of God. Or if baptism is like a wedding, then we are now the bride of Christ. We have done nothing to achieve this. So in moments of stress, guilt, fear, frustration, or despair, I look back to my baptism and say, "I am a baptized man and I live a baptized life."

The same is true of moments of temptation. When I am tempted, I need to look to my baptism and say, "I am a baptized man and I live a baptized life." Once we have been baptized, our thinking needs to catch up with our new status. We are now to live this new reality. We live as those who have died to sin and risen with Christ to a new life. We need to think of ourselves as baptized people. This is the message of Romans 6.

> What shall we say then? Are we to continue in sin that grace may abound? By no means! How can we who died to sin still live in it? Do you not know that all of us who have been baptized into Christ Jesus were baptized into his death? We were buried therefore with him by baptism into death, in order that, just as Christ was raised from the dead by the glory of the Father, we too might walk in newness of life. (6:1–4)

Why should you struggle to stop sinning? Many pastoral issues come down to this question, and Paul's answer is this: You have been baptized. Your baptism is the visible sign that your old self died with Christ and you have risen to a new life. You used to be an in-Adam person, under the power of sin, under the reign of death. But now you are an in-Christ person, set free to live a new life. You are a new person with a new life to live.

Becoming a Christian is more radical than you think, Paul is telling us. It is not just a new set of beliefs or change of opinion. It is even more than a change of allegiance. It is a death and a rebirth! We die with Christ, and we are reborn with Christ.

So baptism is also like a funeral service in which you mark the death of your old self. Indeed, you bury it. That is what happens as you are covered by the water. And then in the next moment—as you emerge from the water—baptism becomes a naming ceremony marking the rebirth of your new self. Like a newborn child, you are given a new name as you are baptized in the name of the Father, the Son, and the Spirit. You become part of the family.

The waters of baptism are both *tomb and womb*—a place for the burial of the old self and a place for the birth of the new self.[2]

Paul goes on in Romans 6, "So you also must consider yourselves dead to sin and alive to God in Christ Jesus" (v. 11). After you get married, you need to act according to the new reality. Imagine someone invites you out for a drink. And you say, "Sure, let's go!" They should respond, "Hang on! Aren't you forgetting something? Remember your wedding day? Count yourself married. Make sure it's okay with your wife." You have to think of yourself in a new way because your status has changed. In the same way, Paul says to baptized Christians, "Count yourselves dead to sin but alive to God in Christ Jesus." Live as baptized people. Your baptism happened in the past. For some of us that was many years ago. But each and every day we are to look back to that moment and remember the reality it marked. Each and every day we are to count ourselves dead to sin and alive to God.

At baptism our identity changes. We know it. Other people know. We enter into a covenant relationship with God. The world turns 180 degrees. That is why Paul keeps pointing people back to their baptism. Here are some examples.

---

2. Cyril of Jerusalem calls the baptism water "both tomb and mother for you." Sermon 2.4, in *The Awe-Inspiring Rites of Initiation: Baptismal Homilies of the Fourth Century*, ed. Edward Yarnold (Slough: St. Paul, 1972), 76.

1 Corinthians 12:12–14

> For just as the [human] body is one and has many members,
> and all the members of the body, though many, are one body,
> so it is with Christ. For in one Spirit we were all baptized
> into one body—Jews or Greeks, slaves or free—and all were
> made to drink of one Spirit. For the body does not consist of
> one member but of many.

Paul's argument is this: A human body has many limbs and organs, which work together. They need one another. In the same way, the church is a body made up of many individual members. And we need one another. We need to work together. But notice the importance of baptism in this argument. Baptism is the sign that we have joined the body. Your baptism marks you out as part of the body of the church. Your status has changed. You are not on your own anymore. You are one of the family.

Galatians 3:26–29

> For in Christ Jesus you are all sons of God, through faith.
> For as many of you as were baptized into Christ have put
> on Christ. There is neither Jew nor Greek, there is neither
> slave nor free, there is no male and female, for you are all
> one in Christ Jesus. And if you are Christ's, then you are
> Abraham's offspring, heirs according to promise.

Some people in Galatia were saying Gentile converts needed to be circumcised because Gentiles were second-class members of God's family. But Paul says, in effect, "You are *all* children of God." The only thing that matters is "faith." What makes us God's children is not our ethnicity or social status or gender, but Christ. How do we know this? Because of baptism. Baptism publicly and officially connects us to Christ. We were baptized *into Christ*. We were clothed *with Christ*.

Colossians 2:11–12

> In him also you were circumcised with a circumcision made without hands, by putting off the body of the flesh, by the circumcision of Christ, having been buried with him in baptism, in which you were also raised with him through faith in the powerful working of God, who raised him from the dead.

People in Colossae were saying you needed to keep the law to conquer the desires of the flesh. Paul says that victory has already happened. Your flesh died with Christ, and you have risen to a new life. How do you know? Because you were baptized. Baptism enacts our dying with Christ and rising with him. We live now in the power of God.

Remodeled on Christ

The Christian life has a distinctive shape to it. It is the shape of the cross and resurrection.

- Jesus says, "If anyone would come after me, let him deny himself and take up his cross daily and follow me. For . . . whoever loses his life for my sake will save it" (Luke 9:23–24).
- Paul says, "We suffer with him in order that we may also be glorified with him" (Rom. 8:17).
- We are "always carrying in the body the death of Jesus, so that the life of Jesus may also be manifested in our bodies" (2 Cor. 4:10).
- Paul's concern, he says, is "that I may know him and the power of his resurrection, and may share his sufferings, becoming like him in his death, that by any means possible I may attain the resurrection from the dead" (Phil. 3:10–11).

- Peter exhorts us, "Rejoice insofar as you share Christ's sufferings, that you may also rejoice and be glad when his glory is revealed" (1 Pet. 4:13).

I could go on with further examples. This is what a Christian is: someone who has died and risen with Christ. This is what the Christian life looks like:

- Death to self and life to God
- Death in us, life in others
- Suffering now followed by eternal glory

Right there at the beginning of our Christian lives, baptism imprints this shape on us. We are buried with Christ as we go under the water, and we rise with Christ as we emerge again. We are those who have died with Christ and risen with Christ. It is like a stamp with a mold that reshapes our lives according to a new design—the design of Christ's death and resurrection. We are remodeled on Christ.

Communion Shapes Our Character

If I threw you a ball, you would almost certainly catch it, especially if you knew it was coming. But consider what is involved in training a robot to catch a ball—all the calculations involved in identifying and then predicting the trajectory of the ball plus all the calculations required to move the robot's hand into place and close its fingers at just the right moment. Yet, when you and I catch a ball, we make none of those calculations. I am told that people with Parkinson's disease who struggle to control their hand movements can nevertheless catch a ball because they do so subconsciously. We do it by *instinct*.

But it is *learned* instinct.

When you first throw a ball to a small child, the child just stands there looking bemused. So you might say, "Put your hands out." Whether the child then catches the ball depends entirely on the accuracy of your throw. Yet the child is the one who gets praised if the ball remains in his or her arms! Children are not born with an innate ability to catch. They learn it. But they learn it without mastering advanced calculus. They are not inputting estimated speeds and angles into a formula to calculate the trajectory as the ball flies through the air. It is learned instinct.

But it is not just catching a ball that works like this.

- How do you type a capital *G* on a computer?
- How do you bring a car to a stop?
- How do you shape an E chord on a guitar?
- How do you find your way to work?

We once thought these things through step-by-step, but now this knowledge has become ingrained. It is imprinted in us. We have done these actions so many times that they have become instinctive. You may even have had to move your hands to consciously answer some of those questions. For example, in an instant I can use a combination of computer keys to move the cursor to the beginning of this document as I type. Yet I cannot tell you offhand what that combination is. I would have to move my fingers into place, watch as I enter the keystrokes, and then tell you. (For the record, I have just done so, and now I can inform you that it's Alt+↖.)

This kind of learned reflex can be reinforced by physical actions. The workers on Japan's rail system repeatedly call out to no one and point to seemingly nothing. A train driver checking his speed, for example, does not simply glance at the dial. The driver points at it and shouts out, "Speed check, 80." When staff check whether the platform is clear, they sweep their arms along their view of the platform, their eyes following their hands, before shouting an all-clear signal. The idea is that associating key tasks with physical movements and vocalizations prevents errors by "raising the consciousness levels of workers." The gestures are not an inherent part of the task. But the physical reinforcement helps ensure each step is complete and accurate. It works. Crazy as this may seem, these apparently pointless gestures have helped to make it one of the safest railway networks in the world. This pointing-and-calling safety method, known as *shisa kanko*, reduces workplace errors by up to 85 percent, according to one 1996 study. A similar system has been adapted for use on New York's MTA subway system. As a result, the number of incorrectly berthed trains has halved.[3]

In *The Road to Wigan Pier*, George Orwell gives an example of how learned instinct can be acquired through an organizational culture and become deeply embedded in our attitudes.

> When I was fourteen or fifteen I was an odious little snob, but no worse than other boys of my own age and class. I suppose there is no place in the world where snobbery is quite so ever-present or where it is cultivated in such refined and subtle forms as in an English public school. Here at least one cannot say that English "education" fails to do its job. You forget your Latin and Greek within a few months of leaving school—I studied Greek for eight or ten years, and now, at thirty-three, I cannot even repeat the Greek alphabet—but your snobbishness, unless you persistently root it out like the bindweed it is, sticks by you till your grave.[4]

---

3. Allan Richarz, "Why Japan's Rail Workers Can't Stop Pointing at Things," *Atlas Obscura*, March 29, 2017, http://www.atlasobscura.com/articles/pointing-and-calling -japan-trains.

4. George Orwell, *The Road to Wigan Pier* (London: Penguin Classics, 2001), 128.

What Orwell learned at school was not just what was taught in his lessons. He was profoundly shaped by the culture of the community in which he lived—in ways that later caused him shame. Indeed, the lessons learned through participating in the school culture were more formative than the lessons learned in the school classroom.

In the same way, Christian formation takes place in more ways than simply through sermons. Lessons learned through participating in the life of the community are often just as formative as lessons learned from the pulpit. For these are the lessons that become habitual and instinctive. This instinctive response (for good or ill) is what we call "character." A godly character is a character that instinctively responds in godly ways. It is the accumulation of repeated gospel thinking, gospel choices, and gospel actions. Godliness becomes our reflexive response to the challenges of life.

And character development does not just happen in lessons. The Lord's Supper is one way in which a gospel life becomes instinctive. The Supper is one of the God-given means through which *we habituate the gospel*. It is a physical gesture, like the Japanese railway's *shisa kanko*, that reinforces Christlike attitudes. As we participate in the drama enacted in the Lord's Supper week after week in the context of the Christian community, the truths it embodies become instinctive. James K. A. Smith comments:

> The tangible display and performance of the gospel in the Lord's Supper is a deeply affecting practice. Its sights and smells, its rhythms and movements, are the sort of thing that seep into our imaginations and become second nature. Just as a song makes words stick in our memory, so the sights, smells, and rhythms of the Eucharist seem to make

the story both come alive and wriggle into our imaginations
in a way that it wouldn't otherwise.[5]

The Lord's Supper is our training ground, a simulation exercise, a role play. Todd Billings does not exaggerate when he says,
"Celebrating the Lord's Supper can change lives."[6]

Let's consider three examples.

1. Participating in Communion Shapes Our Service

Jesus has just shared bread and wine, thereby instituting the
Lord's Supper. Immediately the disciples start arguing about
who is the greatest. Jesus responds by pointing them back to
the Supper: "For who is the greater, one who reclines at table
or one who serves? Is it not the one who reclines at table? But I
am among you as the one who serves" (Luke 22:27). Every time
we take Communion, we are hosted by Christ. The King of the
universe is not being served but is serving. And the bread and
wine point us to the cross, the moment when the one who was
equal with God "humbled himself by becoming obedient to the
point of death" (Phil. 2:8). Not only that, but we also serve one
another. We practice, as it were, the art of service. Every time
we take the Supper, we remember the servant King and serve
one another, and as a result humility and service become a little
bit more instinctive for us. Jesus goes on: "And I assign to you,
as my Father assigned to me, a kingdom, that you may eat and
drink at my table in my kingdom and sit on thrones judging the
twelve tribes of Israel" (Luke 22:29–30). In the bread and wine
we receive a kingdom. The Supper points us to the great eternal
banquet of the Messiah. There is simply no need to fight for

---

5. James K. A. Smith, *Desiring the Kingdom: Worship, Worldview, and Cultural Formation* (Grand Rapids, MI: Baker, 2009), 198.

6. J. Todd Billings, *Remembrance, Communion, and Hope: Rediscovering the Gospel at
the Lord's Table* (Grand Rapids, MI: Eerdmans, 2018), 7.

positions of honor when you have already been seated at the Lord's Supper, feasting with the King.

One occasion may not change us—as the disciples proved at the Last Supper. But every time we take Communion, we are learning how to serve, and we are learning this from the King himself.

2. Participating in Communion Shapes Our Gratitude

Let's consider another example. One of the terms for the Lord's Supper is the "Eucharist." It comes from the Greek word meaning "give thanks." Every account of the Supper in the New Testament includes giving thanks. Luke's account, for example, says, "He took bread, and when he had given thanks, he broke it and gave it to them" (Luke 22:19). Paul describes the cup as "the cup of thanksgiving" (1 Cor. 10:16 NIV). The Lord's Supper is an act of thanksgiving. We learn in the Eucharist to receive the bread and wine as signs of God's generosity. The primary focus for that thanksgiving is the self-giving of God in Christ. But this act trains us to be grateful people and give thanks to God for all his gifts. B. A. Gerrish say that the central theme of Calvin's understanding of the Supper is the Father's generosity and our grateful response. But not only is this the theme of the Supper, Gerrish argues; it is also the central theme of Calvin's theology. "The holy banquet is simply the liturgical enactment of the theme of grace and gratitude that lies at the heart of Calvin's entire theology."[7]

Think what it does for a community if one of the rhythms of its life is a regular act of thanksgiving. What kind of people will they be? They will see God as a generous Father. They will see the world as his generous gift. They will receive it with a sense of wonder. They will be full of gratitude. And seeing themselves

---

7. B. A. Gerrish, *Grace and Gratitude: The Eucharistic Theology of John Calvin* (Eugene, OR: Wipf and Stock, 1993), 20.

as recipients of God's generosity will encourage them to be generous people. Thinking of God as a generous Father will free them from the need to hold on to what they possess. This is how the first church was described: "Day by day . . . breaking bread in their homes, they received their food with glad and generous hearts" (Acts 2:46). These attitudes are learned and reinforced and celebrated every time we participate in the Eucharist, the thanksgiving. We live a eucharistic life, a life of gratitude and generosity shaped by the Supper.

3. Participating in Communion Reshapes Your View of the World

It is often said that nothing magical happens when we take Communion. I understand what is meant by this. I have said it myself a number of times in this book. There is no conjuring trick in which bread becomes flesh.

But have the people who say this never seen rain? Rain can be wholly explained in terms of the water cycle. But is it not a little bit magical? Water is falling from the sky! We need water for life, and God has arranged the world so that it falls down out of the sky on us. This life-giving elixir is delivered literally out of the blue.

My point is this. We live in a magical world which teems with God's grace. Creation is itself an act of grace. God did not have to make the world. There was no lack in himself that required the creation of a world. He was not lonely so that he created someone to talk to. The Trinity is a perfect, complete, self-sufficient community of joy. No, God created out of love. And what he created is full of beauty and wonder. It is a sign of glory and generosity. Creation is an act of grace that is full of grace.

And at the center of this world of grace is the Lord's Table, given to us as a symbol and sign of our grace-filled world. The Lord's Table is supposed to be the tip of the iceberg. This is the moment when we point to bread and wine and say, "There is grace." But this moment is given to remind us that *every* moment is full of grace. It reminds us that this world is porous, a world in which the heavenly and the earthly intersect. And it reminds us that our God is not the god of the deists, who merely looks on from afar; our God is both transcendent over our world and immanent within our world.

If you let the Lord's Supper change you, it will.

Imagine doing an internship with someone you admire. Some of you may have had that opportunity. Week by week you talk together and that person shapes your thinking. But not just your thinking. You see your mentor in action and are invited to join in the activity. As a result, your whole character is shaped.

Communion is the ultimate internship. We are interns with Jesus himself. Week by week we hear his words. But we also see him in action as the Communion meal reenacts his story. And he invites us to participate in his actions. He invites us to join him in serving others. He imprints the shape of his death and resurrection on our lives. It is profoundly formative.

Each time we take Communion,

- we act as sinners in need of grace;
- we act as children adopted by God;
- we act as liberated people, redeemed by the blood of Christ;
- we act as the bride of Christ, bound to him in a marriage covenant;
- we act as a community joined together by the cross;
- we act as participants in Christ, dying to self and rising to a new life.

"Act" is a good word. Baptism and Communion are like minidramas. And we are not just in the audience; we are part of the cast.

We do not look on from afar, merely learning information. We participate in the drama. We live in character. And as we live in character, we become the characters we should be—the characters we already are by grace. We learn our lines and then we learn to improvise. So, as we go from the Supper into the world, we are more equipped to play our part as men and women in Christ.

But this drama is not make-believe. We reenact the story of Jesus.

- We act out what really happened in history in the death and resurrection of Jesus.
- We act out what will really happen at the end of history when the bride of Christ feasts with the bridegroom.
- We act out what really is happening now in heaven as Christ welcomes us into his presence.

This shaping of our character happens more than we realize. But it is not automatic. We need to be thoughtful. Word and sacrament belong together. I realize actions can lose their meaning. But then so can words. We talk about empty actions, but we also talk about empty words. The challenge is to fill baptism and Communion with meaning so they become meaning-full and therefore meaningful. As you share Communion, think about specific ways in which the story retold and embodied in Communion comforts or challenges you at this moment.

So as you approach Communion week by week, think about the story it tells and think of yourself as a participant in that story. It is already your story if you are a Christian. *But Christ in his kindness, knowing how frail we are, how battered by life, how prone to temptation, has given us baptism and Communion so we feel it is our story and so we inhabit the story.* He has given us Communion so we learn to play our part not as hopeless rebels or as self-righteous Pharisees, but as blood-bought children.

A BAPTIZED PEOPLE

You can read your Bible on your own (though it is better to do it with others when you get the chance). You can pray on your own (though, again, it is better to do it with others if you can). You can worship God on your own (though, guess what, it is better to do it with others). But you cannot be baptized or take Communion on your own. Baptism and Communion are communal acts.

It is not just that you need other people to be baptized and take Communion. There is a sense in which the Christian community is formed by baptism and Communion. Baptism brings the church into existence, and Communion sustains its communal life. Thomas Cranmer began the article on the sacraments in his 1552 Forty-Two Articles, which were later revised into the Anglican Church's Thirty-Nine Articles, with the words "Our Lord Jesus Christ has knit together a company of new people with Sacraments" (§26).

A Community Formed by Baptism
On the day of Pentecost, after Peter had preached to the crowd, "those who received his word were baptized, and there were

added that day about three thousand souls" (Acts 2:41). Baptism and joining the church go together. To be baptized is to be added to the church; and you join the church by being baptized. This pattern is repeated throughout the book of Acts.

Baptism is how the church is defined and how membership of the church is defined. The church is *a baptized people*. Just as Israel was the people who had passed through the waters of the Red Sea with Moses (1 Cor. 10:2), so the church is the people who have passed through the water of baptism with Jesus. Paul says, "For in one Spirit we were all baptized into one body—Jews or Greeks, slaves or free—and all were made to drink of one Spirit" (1 Cor. 12:13). He uses similar language in Galatians 3:26–28: "For in Christ Jesus you are all sons of God, through faith. For as many of you as were baptized into Christ have put on Christ. There is neither Jew nor Greek, there is neither slave nor free, there is no male and female, for you are all one in Christ Jesus." All our old loyalties and identities dissolve in the waters of baptism and are replaced with a new allegiance: to Christ and his people. Again, in Ephesians 4:3–4, Paul calls on us to be "eager to maintain the unity of the Spirit in the bond of peace." The reason is this: "There is one body and one Spirit—just as you were called to the one hope that belongs to your call—one Lord, one faith, one baptism, one God and Father of all." The church is one body because we share (among other things) one baptism.

There is only one door into the church, and that is the font or baptistery.

There are legal and practical reasons why many churches have a formal membership list. But you do not become a member of the church when your name is added to a list. The list will simply be an administrative and legal convenience. You become a member of the church when you are baptized. If you are moving to another city and you have already been baptized, then you start being part of a new church when you start taking Communion, because Communion is how we express our ongoing belonging to the church.

A Community Formed by the Supper

Just as baptism is a community-forming act, so is Communion. There is a clue in the name! The Lord's Supper is an act of Communion. It is an act of communion with Christ (as we saw in chapter 3), but it is also an act of communion with one another. In Communion we enact community.

Indeed, the community and the Communion meal are created by one another. The community creates the Supper in the sense that without the community the bread and wine would be just that. A table with bread and wine, however beautifully decorated, is not the Lord's Supper. It becomes the Lord's Supper only when there are people gathered around the table. The bread and wine take on meaning in the context of the community of faith. This is why you cannot take Communion on your own.

At the same time the Supper creates the community. Consider Paul's words in 1 Corinthians 10:17: "Because there is one bread, we who are many are one body, for we all partake of the one bread." Why are we one body? Because we all share the one loaf. How is it that this diverse group of people from a variety of generations, ethnicities, and social classes comes together to form one church? How can a group of individuals—"we, who are many," as Paul puts it—with different priorities and personalities share a common life? How is it that your church, with all its differences and difficulties, functions as a family? Because we all share the one loaf.

At an objective level, what creates Christian community is the death and resurrection of Jesus. Paul says, "Christ loved the church and gave himself up for her" (Eph. 5:25). Christ did not die in order to collect an assortment of detached individuals. He died to create and redeem the church. Individuals are saved when, by faith, they become part of the people for whom Christ died. In Ephesians 2, Paul describes how the cross has broken down the dividing wall of hostility between Jew and Gentile. We are humbled by the cross so that any social superiority dissolves. The old allegiances of race, class, and gender are relativized by our new identity as God's family. That is at an objective level. Through the cross we are a family. It's a fact. Nothing we do can add to or subtract from this reality.

But church does not always *feel* like family. After all, we remain a diverse group of individuals with our different backgrounds and personalities. Inevitably, tensions arise. *So Christ in his kindness, knowing how frail we are, how battered by life, how battered by one another we can be, has given us the Lord's Supper* to help us *feel* like a family and to help us *live* as a family.

The Lord's Supper creates Christian community at a *subjective* or existential level. Our divisions and our differences begin to melt as we eat (1) together, (2) with a focus on the cross, (3) in the Spirit-enabled presence of our Lord and Savior.

This is why what was happening in the church in Corinth so offends Paul. Instead of *melting away* their divisions, their Communion meals were *accentuating* their divisions. Paul has to say to them: "But in the following instructions I do not commend you, because when you come together it is not for the better but for the worse. For, in the first place, when you come together as a church, I hear that there are divisions among you. And I believe it in part" (1 Cor. 11:17–18).

Wayne A. Meeks explains that in the culture of the day it was common for banquets to be "occasions for the conspicuous display of social distance and even for humiliation of the clients of the rich, by means of the quality and quantity of food provided to different tables."[1] A larger home would have a private dining room or triclinium that could accommodate up to a dozen guests. You can imagine how a wealthy host might invite high-status church members to eat in this private room. Meanwhile the low-status members would be left to eat in the open courtyard or atrium—if indeed they arrived on time, having only been released by their employers or owners late in the day. It seems the wealthy in Corinth were using the Lord's Supper in this way to highlight their social superiority. An expression of division and distinction was their goal.

They were basically saying: "This talk of being one in Christ is all well and good. But obviously in practice I can't eat with *those* people. No one could expect that. There have to be some differences between us—some distinctions of class and rank. We have to make some distinction between citizens and slaves, between Romans and barbarians. So we'll have the Lord's Supper, but we'll eat first, and we'll eat with our peers in the private dining room."

Today we might say, "I'm a big fan of community, but obviously I can't open my home to people who are mentally ill or immigrants or on welfare." Or maybe we would say: "I want to be in a small group with people like me. I don't want to be stuck with a load of old fogies or endure the clamor of small children. That doesn't fit my image of community." Or maybe we'd say, "Don't expect me to sit next to *those* people—not after what they've done to me." We might not *say* these things, but we can think them. Or perhaps the most likely option is that we formally assent to unity in Christ across barriers of race and class, but in practice all the people in our church with whom we spend time are like us.

---

1. Wayne A. Meeks, *The First Urban Christians: The Social World of the Apostle Paul* (New Haven, CT: Yale University Press, 1983), 68.

Paul responds in 1 Corinthians 11:19 with irony: "No doubt there have to be differences among you to show which of you have God's approval" (NIV). What he is saying, in effect, is this: "You're right. Differences are revealed around the Communion table. But not the differences you think. Communion is not about social superiors and inferiors. The real difference revealed there is the only one that really matters: those who understand the gospel and those who don't." Indeed, he goes on to say that ultimately the difference is between those who are nourished by Christ around the table and those who eat and drink judgment on themselves (1 Cor. 11:27–30).

Paul sums up his rebuke in 1 Corinthians 11:20: "When you come together, it is not the Lord's supper that you eat." The meal they selfishly enjoy does not proclaim the Lord's death. Paul has to take them back to the gospel—which the Supper is meant to embody—in the well-known words of verses 23–26. We proclaim the death of Jesus by eating together as a community reconciled through the cross. *The* people *around the table proclaim Christ's death just as much as the bread and wine on the table.*

So do not close your eyes as you receive the bread and wine, as if the Supper is a private transaction between you and God. Open your eyes and look around the room. See the body of Christ (represented by your local church) formed by the shared experience of the body of Christ (represented by the one loaf). Look at each person receiving Christ in bread and wine. Maybe you wish there were different people in your church; perhaps you wish some awkward customers would leave; perhaps you wish more people like you would join. But the people around you are the people Christ has chosen, and these are the people for whom he died. And here they are, sharing with you in his grace.

In Communion we are reminded of our sin, and so our superiorities dissolve. At the same time, we see that our fellow Christians are saints bought with the blood of Christ. The price tag of their clothes is irrelevant once you have read the price tag of their lives, which is the precious blood of Christ. What the world thinks of them is eclipsed by what God thinks of them, and his welcome is symbolized in the bread and wine you see them receiving. They are children of God, and therefore they are our brothers and sisters. The family that eats together stays together!

So the Supper declares the death of Jesus not just in the symbolism of bread and wine but also in the effect it creates: the reconciled family of God, eating together as the sign of reconciliation.

A number of implications flow from the communal nature of Communion.

1. The Supper Is a Means of Reconciliation

In the Sermon on the Mount, Jesus says: "So if you are offering your gift at the altar and there remember that your brother has something against you, leave your gift there before the altar and go. First be reconciled to your brother, and then come and offer your gift" (Matt. 5:23–24; see also 6:14–15). We no longer have an altar, because Christ, our Passover Lamb, has been sacrificed for us. But we do remember his sacrifice at the Communion table. So this has rightly been reinterpreted, after the cross, as a call to be reconciled before taking Communion. In some church traditions this is enacted in the sharing of the peace.

First Corinthians 11, as we have seen, is a warning not to take Communion without being reconciled. In Corinth this had led to some people becoming ill under God's judgment, even to deaths (v. 30). So Paul warns the Corinthians in verses 27–29:

Whoever, therefore, eats the bread or drinks the cup of the Lord in an unworthy manner will be guilty concerning the body and blood of the Lord. Let a person examine himself, then, and so eat of the bread and drink of the cup. For anyone who eats and drinks without discerning the body eats and drinks judgment on himself.

The point is not that we have to be worthy of receiving bread and wine by being good people. After all, the Supper is an invitation to sinners to come to receive grace. Instead, what makes us "unworthy" in 1 Corinthians 11 is a sin against "the body," that is, against people in the church. It is not a sense of *inferiority* that makes us unworthy to receive Communion—in fact, that is one of the main requirements! What makes us unworthy is a false sense of *superiority*. What makes Communion a denial of the cross rather than a celebration of the cross is any refusal to be reconciled, to seek forgiveness, or to forgive. James M. Hamilton cautions us, "Those who partake unworthily identify themselves with those who crucified Christ rather than with those for whom He was crucified."[2]

Christ has built into the rhythms of the common life of the local church a regular prompt to pursue reconciliation. This is so striking. Week by week, month by month, there is a moment when we are given a fresh call to forbear and forgive. I wonder if there is anyone with whom you need to talk before you next take Communion.

But Communion is not simply a *prompt* toward reconciliation. It also gives us the *resources* for reconciliation. For in the bread and wine we are reminded of God's justice and God's grace.

---

2. James M. Hamilton Jr., "The Lord's Supper in Paul: An Identity-Forming Proclamation of the Gospel," in *The Lord's Supper: Remembering and Proclaiming Christ until He Comes*, ed. Thomas R. Schreiner and Matthew R. Crawford (Nashville: B&H, 2010), 93.

2. The Supper Is a Means of Church Discipline

The opposite is also true. If the Supper can express reconciliation, then it can also express censure. First Corinthians 5 is a call to exercise church discipline through excommunication (in this case against someone who is having an affair with his stepmother). Paul says that for the sake of the offender, the church, and Christ's reputation, the Corinthian church must act. "When you are assembled in the name of the Lord Jesus and my spirit is present, with the power of our Lord Jesus, you are to deliver this man to Satan for the destruction of the flesh, so that his spirit may be saved in the day of the Lord" (5:4–5).

But what are the practical consequences of this? What form does excommunication take? Paul goes on to say:

> I wrote to you in my letter not to associate with sexually immoral people—not at all meaning the sexually immoral of this world, or the greedy and swindlers, or idolaters, since then you would need to go out of the world. But now I am writing to you not to associate with anyone who bears the name of brother if he is guilty of sexual immorality or greed, or is an idolater, reviler, drunkard, or swindler—not even to eat with such a one. (5:9–11)

The one practical difference that excommunication makes is exclusion from the table. Is this table an ordinary meal or a Communion meal? Perhaps it is both; perhaps it does not matter. Both signify reconciliation. But there can be no expression of reconciliation until there is repentance.

The "keys of the kingdom." When Peter confesses that Jesus is the Christ, Jesus says in response:

> Blessed are you, Simon Bar-Jonah! For flesh and blood has not revealed this to you, but my Father who is in heaven.

> And I tell you, you are Peter, and on this rock I will build
> my church, and the gates of hell shall not prevail against
> it. I will give you the keys of the kingdom of heaven, and
> whatever you bind on earth shall be bound in heaven, and
> whatever you loose on earth shall be loosed in heaven.
> (Matt. 16:17–19)

Previous generations spoke of "the power of the keys." The
church has power to bind and loose. What does this mean? It
is a strong statement, for it says that what happens on earth affects what happens in heaven.

The "keys" and proclamation. The first place to go to explore
the power of the keys is John 20, where the risen Christ meets
his disciples:

> Jesus said to them again, "Peace be with you. As the Father
> has sent me, even so I am sending you." And when he had
> said this, he breathed on them and said to them, "Receive
> the Holy Spirit. If you forgive the sins of any, they are forgiven them; if you withhold forgiveness from any, it is withheld." (John 20:21–23)

Here the power of the keys is linked to our proclamation. Jesus
says he will empower his people with the Holy Spirit—a promised that was fulfilled at Pentecost. As a result, our Spirit-empowered preaching determines people's eternal fate. If they
respond to our proclamation with faith and repentance, then
their sins are forgiven. But if they reject our proclamation, then
they are not forgiven. What happens on earth affects what happens in heaven. It adds great weight to our evangelism. Eternal
destinies are being determined as you talk about Jesus with
your friends and colleagues. The power of the keys is exercised
through gospel proclamation.

The "keys" and church discipline. But there is more to it than that. In Matthew 18, Jesus uses the same language of binding and loosing.

> If your brother sins against you, go and tell him his fault, between you and him alone. If he listens to you, you have gained your brother. But if he does not listen, take one or two others along with you, that every charge may be established by the evidence of two or three witnesses. If he refuses to listen to them, tell it to the church. And if he refuses to listen even to the church, let him be to you as a Gentile and a tax collector. Truly, I say to you, whatever you bind on earth shall be bound in heaven, and whatever you loose on earth shall be loosed in heaven. Again I say to you, if two of you agree on earth about anything they ask, it will be done for them by my Father in heaven. For where two or three are gathered in my name, there am I among them. (vv. 15–20)

What Jesus is describing here is church discipline. We often associate church discipline with excommunication. But it is important to notice that it does not start there. It starts with a gentle one-to-one rebuke (Matt. 18:15). Only if this is ignored or rebuffed does it escalate. One reason church discipline today is frequently ineffective is that these early stages are often neglected. We avoid confrontation until the problem has grown and excommunication has become the only option.

Nevertheless, though church discipline does not begin with excommunication, excommunication is where it ultimately ends if there is no repentance. The lovely little assurance "where two or three are gathered in my name, there am I among them," which we sometimes use when our prayer meetings are low on numbers, is actually a promise given in a judicial context. Jesus promises that when we enact church discipline, "whatever you bind on earth shall be bound in heaven, and whatever you loose on earth shall be loosed in heaven"— words similar to those he said to Peter in Matthew 16.

We find it too hard to get our heads around this because we are so individualistic and so voluntaristic—we assume everyone acts for themselves and cannot be shaped by other people. These verses sound like they invest huge power in the church. And indeed they do. Perhaps we instinctively ask, "What if the church makes a mistake?" Then we can trust the Judge of all the earth to do right. He has not bound himself to uphold faulty decisions. The assumption in Matthew 16 and 18, albeit an implicit one, is that the church is acting rightly. But we must not let these kinds of questions obscure the fact that the church acts in a judicial way, or better still, a covenantal way, with far-reaching consequences.

The "keys" and baptism and Communion. The power of the keys is linked to baptism and Communion.[3] Baptism and Communion are how this power is exercised. Again, the parallel with marriage will help. A wedding does not make you fall in love. But a wedding does give your love covenantal status. It binds your spouse to you in a lifelong commitment. It protects your love from the ups and downs of your emotions. Indeed, it is a covenant with legal status and therefore requires a legal process to undo.

In the same way, baptism does not make you a Christian. But baptism does give your faith covenantal status. It binds Christ to you in an eternal commitment. It changes your identity. Its covenant commitments protect your faith from the ups and downs of your emotions. Indeed, it is a covenant with a kind

---

3. See, for example, John Calvin, *Institutes of the Christian Religion*, ed. John T. Mc-Neill, trans. Ford Lewis Battles, Library of Christian Classics 20–21 (Philadelphia: Westminster, 1960), 4.15.4.

of legal status that requires a legal process to undo—the process in which the church exercises "the power of the keys." Just as Communion is an act of covenant renewal, so the denial of Communion is an act of covenant censure.

3. The Supper Is a Means of Evangelism

Baptism is how we express our *joining* the church, and Communion is how we express our *belonging to* the church. This means baptism goes before Communion. You join before you belong.[4]

Why do Christians believe sex belongs within marriage? Because you cannot express covenantal love in sex until you have first made a covenant commitment in marriage. In the same way, you cannot express belonging to the church in Communion until you have first joined the church in baptism. Taking Communion before being baptized is like having sex before marriage. You are trying to grab the benefits of a covenant relationship without the commitment.

Think of it like this. Whatever reason someone gives for not being baptized is a reason for not taking Communion. Or, to turn it round, whatever reason someone gives for taking Communion is a reason for first being baptized.

Think what this means for children growing up in a credobaptist home. They should not take Communion without first being baptized. "Why can't they take Communion," you might ask, "since they have put their faith in Jesus?" Because if they have put their faith in Jesus, they should first be baptized. "But they're not ready to be baptized," you say. I am not sure what that readiness involves since there is no other requirement than faith in Jesus. But if they are not prepared to be baptized, then they are not ready to take Communion.

---

4. See J. Todd Billings, *Remembrance, Communion, and Hope: Rediscovering the Gospel at the Lord's Table* (Grand Rapids, MI: Eerdmans, 2018), 150–55.

Or think what this means to those exploring the Christian faith. Maybe they ask whether they can take Communion. What do you do? You talk about baptism. Suppose they then say, "I'm not ready to make that commitment yet." Then you say: "That's fine. You're welcome to take part in our community life. But baptism and Communion go together. If you're not ready to express your connection to Christ in baptism, then you're not ready to express your commitment to Christ in Communion."

Or perhaps some have attended a church for a while without joining. They have heard the gospel preached and seen it in the lives of their friends. Maybe they have come to realize that they, too, now believe in Jesus. Maybe they have begun to express that by taking Communion. Then they should be baptized. If they want to express belonging to the Christian community, then they should first join the Christian community by being baptized.

This means baptism and Communion are really important in evangelism.

We want unbelievers to be involved in our shared life as the church, because we want them to hear the gospel and see it lived out. So we invite people to be involved in everything we do together. In this context, Communion becomes really important. It is the one moment in our life together when we draw the line. One of the reasons God gave the sacraments, says the Westminster Confession, is "to put a visible difference between those that belong unto the church, and the rest of the world" (27.1). Francis Turretin says the sacraments are badges God uses to "distinguish and separate his people from the rest of the world."[5] This makes Communion an opportunity to call people to faith and repentance.

---

5. Francis Turretin, *Institutes of Elenctic Theology*, trans. George Musgrave Giger, ed. James T. Dennison Jr., vol. 3 (Phillipsburg, NJ: P&R, 1997), 337.

Some people hide Communion away by celebrating it in a separate meeting so no one is offended by their exclusion. But this is a missed opportunity. Whatever process you have for "guarding the table" (that is, ensuring that only baptized Christians take Communion), you can use Communion as an opportunity to talk to people about their commitment to Christ and his people.

As you celebrate Communion, invite all those who have been baptized to participate. Suggest that those who have not been baptized simply remain in their seats or pass on the bread and wine without any embarrassment. If you notice people who have not been baptized taking the bread and wine, there is no need to dive across the room and snatch it from their hands. They are not about to eat poison or corrupt the cup. For them it is just bread and wine. But use this as an opportunity to talk with them about their commitment to Christ and his people. You might say: "I saw you taking Communion. That's an expression of faith in Christ and union with Christ. Is that a step you've taken? I'd love to hear about it." If you're in a credobaptist church, then you might also add, "And if you're united to Christ by faith, then we should baptize you." If they are not ready to do that, then they are not ready to take Communion.

Maybe you can see my logic, but you think my position is a bit hard-line. Maybe you shrink from excluding people from Communion because they have not expressed commitment to Christ and his church through baptism. Maybe that feels unloving or unwelcoming. But the fact is that those who refuse to be baptized are the ones deciding that they are not part of the Christian community. All we are doing is asking them to be consistent—and to reconsider.

More importantly, including someone in Communion who is not willing to be baptized sends a dangerous message.

It allows someone to think he or she is okay with God when in fact the person has not turned to him in faith, expressed in baptism, and is not living in obedience to him. By all means involve such a person in everything you do as a church, but with one exception—Communion. You may feel you want to be loving by accepting people to the Supper. But there is nothing loving about giving people false assurance. The most loving thing we can do is call people to faith and repentance.

To summarize, we should encourage anyone and everyone to share in the life of our churches. But there is one moment where we draw a line in the sand. That moment is Communion. This is the moment where we highlight the fact that there are people who are in Christ and people outside of Christ. In this way Communion creates a great opportunity to call people to faith and repentance.

CONCLUSION

Re-enchanting the World

Evangelical Christians today think of transubstantiation as too superstitious. When the priest lifts up the bread, he says, *Hoc est corpus meum*, the Latin for "This is my body." It is often said that this led to the expression *hocus-pocus*, which we use colloquially for a spell or for something that is bogus. This derivation is disputed. But it reflects the fact that transubstantiation feels to us like a superstitious magic trick.

Yet Martin Luther rejected transubstantiation not because it was too *superstitious* but because it was too *rational*. And it is illuminating to reflect on these contrasting concerns.

It was Thomas Aquinas who gave fullest expression to transubstantiation. Let me explain his argument. Imagine you are meeting me for the first time in forty years. Four decades ago I was a child. I was a foot shorter, skinny, and energetic. My voice had not broken. Now I am taller and sporting the first signs of grey hair. My appearance has changed beyond recognition. But you would not claim I was a different person. I am still Tim Chester. All the particulars of my appearance have changed—height, weight, hair color, skin tone, waist line. But my essential self remains the same. What Aquinas argued was this: that is what happens in Communion *in reverse*. He used categories from the Greek philosopher Aristotle. Aristotle distinguished between the "accidents" of something (what we have called the particulars—in my case, things like size, hair color, and so on) and the "substance" (what we have called the essence— my essential self). Aquinas applied this to Communion. All the accidents or particulars of the bread remain the same—its taste, appearance, texture, and so forth. But its substance or essence changes—hence the term "transubstantiation." Aquinas reasoned:

> The substance of the bread or wine, after the consecration, remains neither under the sacramental species, nor elsewhere; yet it does not follow that it is annihilated; for it is changed into the body of Christ. . . . It is evident to sense that all the accidents of the bread and wine remain after the consecration. And this is reasonably done by Divine providence. First of all, because it is not customary, but horrible, for men to eat human flesh, and to drink blood. And therefore Christ's flesh and blood are set before us to be partaken of under the species of those things which are the more commonly used by men, namely, bread and wine.[1]

This is really clever. *Too* clever for Luther. In Luther's mind it drains the mystery out of the Supper. It is the vaunted triumph of human reason to explain the mystery of the presence of Christ in Communion. Luther speaks of "the Aristotelian church," implying that the Catholic position is too influenced by Aristotle:

---

1. Thomas Aquinas, *Summa theologica*, 2nd ed., trans. the Fathers of the English Dominican Province, 1920, III, Q. 75, Arts. 3, 5, http://www.newadvent.org/summa, accessed January 12, 2019.

What shall we say when Aristotle and these human doctrines are made to be arbiters of such lofty and divine matters? Why do we not put aside such curiosity and cling simply to the words of Christ, willing to remain in ignorance of what takes place here and content that the real body of Christ is present by virtue of the words? Or is it necessary to comprehend the manner of the divine working in every detail? . . . Let us not dabble too much in philosophy. . . . For my part, if I cannot fathom how the bread is the body of Christ, yet I will take my reason captive to the obedience of Christ and, clinging simply to his words, firmly believe not only that the body of Christ is in the bread, but that the bread is the body of Christ. . . . What does it matter if philosophy cannot fathom this? The Holy Spirit is greater than Aristotle. . . . Even though philosophy cannot grasp this, faith grasps it nonetheless. And the authority of God's Word is greater than the capacity of our intellect to grasp it.[2]

Luther agreed that Christ is present in Communion. Indeed, he agreed (wrongly in my view, as we saw in chapter 3) that Christ is physically present. But Luther said we cannot describe how this happens. Our reason is inadequate, and instead we receive it from the word by faith.

But consider the contrast between Luther's reaction to transubstantiation and that of evangelicals today. Luther thought it is too rational, and evangelicals think it is too superstitious. What is going on?

Carl Trueman emphasizes that Luther was a thoroughly medieval man.[3] Indeed, we might say Luther was the last medieval

---

2. Martin Luther, "The Babylonian Captivity of the Church," in *The Annotated Luther*, vol. 3, *Church and Sacraments*, ed. Paul W. Robinson (Minneapolis: Fortress, 2016), 31, 36, 37.

3. Carl R. Trueman, *Luther on the Christian Life: Cross and Freedom* (Wheaton, IL: Crossway, 2015), 22–23, 81.

man. It was Luther who unleashed the changes that led to modernity, but he himself remained firmly embedded in the medieval world. "His world was one where the Devil walked abroad, where the supernatural permeated the natural."[4] Luther assumed that the world in which he lived was porous, surrounded by magic, spirits, demons, spells—but also by the mysterious presence of God in bread and wine.

But if this contrast between our different critiques of transubstantiation (too rational versus too superstitious) shows that Luther was a medieval man shaped by his times, it also shows that *we* are modern people shaped by *our* times. Modern people live in what we think of as a closed universe, in which we do not expect divine intervention. Even those who expect frequent miracles have a modern worldview, because they see God's intervention in our world as the exception. This lukewarm expectation exposes our modernity, the way we are entrapped by our culture.

This brings us back to René Descartes. As we saw in the introduction, another characteristic of the modern worldview is a gap between body and mind. Ever since Descartes said, "I think, therefore I am," our minds have had priority. We think of our essential selves as "brains in a vat" looking out on the world—including our own bodies. And so we assume that it is we who attribute or give meaning to objects. This perspective then shapes the way we view Communion. Meaning resides in us rather than in the bread and wine or any objective reality that is taking place at the Communion meal. So we might characterize Zwingli as the first modern man. Luther and Zwingli came to their Reformation convictions from very different directions. Zwingli was part of the new humanist movement (in a way that

4. Trueman, *Luther on the Christian Life*, 23.

was not true of Luther). So Zwingli sees Communion primarily as a memorial.

The Canadian philosopher Charles Taylor argues that one reason why secularization has taken hold is that we no longer believe in an enchanted world. We live in a closed world, what Taylor calls "the immanent frame."[5] In the medieval world, events were routinely interpreted as direct interventions of God or the devil. In the modern world, everything is traced back to natural causes. Natural causes are the sum total of causation in our closed world. They are all that count. Diseases are no longer seen as acts of judgment; accidents are no longer attributed to demonic activity; the body is no longer ensouled. Natural explanations have replaced spiritual or magical explanations. In the medieval world human space was enclosed within other realms—humanity was part of a layered cosmos in which the earthly and heavenly interacted. But in modernity this world is all there is. Indeed, we now talk of the "universe"—"everything in one"—because other realms have been stripped away. And, so, meaning is found entirely *within* the world (even if someone stills regards that world as created by God).

We cannot go back to the medieval world—we know too much about our world and the way it works. We know that lightning is caused by the release of electrical charges in clouds. We know that sicknesses are caused by viral and bacterial infections.

But what we as Christians need to emphasize is that we still live in a world in which God actively and routinely intervenes. He intervenes *through* natural causes (and occasionally apart from natural causes through miracles). We need to see natural causes as the instruments of God. We need to see the world as *a providential cosmos*. That allows us to re-enchant the world.

---

5. Charles Taylor, *A Secular Age* (Cambridge, MA: Harvard University Press, 2007), chap. 15.

Our world is full of wonder, meaning, and divine activity. It is full of opportunities to interact with, and therefore enjoy Communion with, the triune God. It is a world in which heaven and earth intersect, and in which our actions matter for eternity.

And the Lord's Supper is the moment, above all, in which this is seen to take place. It is the sign or pointer to the enchantment of the *whole* world, to God's presence in *all* things. What Calvin offers us is a biblical worldview that bridges the gap between the medieval and modern worldviews with an emphasis on the providence of God and the presence of Christ *through the Holy Spirit.*

Charles Taylor describes our secular age as "haunted," whether by the ghosts of a lost history or by the ghosts of a missing metaphysical Other. People still live with glimpses of transcendence. For honest people, this creates what Taylor calls "cross-pressures," opposing currents of transcendence and immanence.[6] Both belief and unbelief are fraught and fragile.

Communion offers the possibility of re-enchanting our world—a moment of transcendence, a meeting of heaven and earth, a glimpse beyond the immanent frame that would otherwise enclose our view of the world. God's immanence in the world through the Spirit in Communion points us beyond this material world to the transcendence of God.

---

6. Taylor, *A Secular Age*, chap. 16.

GENERAL INDEX

SCRIPTURE INDEX

Also Available from Tim Chester